Presented To:

_____

From:

_____

Date:

_____

THE
word OF
knowledge
in action ↗

THE
word OF
knowledge
in action ↗

A PRACTICAL GUIDE FOR
THE SUPERNATURAL CHURCH

art thomas

DESTINY IMAGE® PUBLISHERS, INC.
P.O. Box 310, Shippensburg, PA 17257-0310
"Speaking to the Purposes of God for This Generation and for the Generations to Come."

This book and all other Destiny Image, Revival Press, MercyPlace, Fresh Bread, Destiny Image Fiction, and Treasure House books are available at Christian bookstores and distributors worldwide.

For a U.S. bookstore nearest you, call 1-800-722-6774.
For more information on foreign distributors, call 717-532-3040.
Reach us on the Internet: www.destinyimage.com.

ISBN 13 TP: 978-0-7684-3776-8
ISBN 13 HC: 978-0-7684-3777-5
ISBN 13 LP: 978-0-7684-3778-2
ISBN 13 Ebook: 978-0-7684-8997-2

For Worldwide Distribution, Printed in the U.S.A.
1 2 3 4 5 6 7 8 9 10 11 / 13 12 11

dedication

I dedicate this book to my firstborn baby, Josiah Samuel. You will have been born just a month before this book goes into print. Surely, your Father in Heaven loves you and has provided for your mother and me with the timing of this book. May the Lord continue to sing blessing over your life. I welcome you into this world and affirm you as my son. You are a blessing.

acknowledgments

Robin, my amazing wife—thank you for standing by me and speaking prophetic destiny into my life. You are a constant encouragement and a powerful spiritual partner in ministry. Thank you for teaching me about the simplicity of faith in God and of divine healing. I am so blessed to have you in my life, and I look forward to all that God has in store for the rest of our lives together. I love you.

Wilmer Singleton—thank you for looking into my manuscript and seeing God's potential for it. You've been a real blessing in bringing this project into print.

John Loren Sandford—thank you for the extensive edit of my book and all your insights and encouragement. It is an honor to have had you speak into this project with such wisdom, knowledge, and Spirit-filled experience.

Dan Vander Velde—thank you for having the patience and spiritual vision to walk an overzealous young man with crazy ideas through the process of inner healing and sanctification. I wouldn't look nearly as much like Jesus if it weren't for the years of your life that you poured into me with wisdom and maturity. This book is as much your accomplishment as it is mine.

Brooks McElhenny—thank you for taking a risk on a nameless 23-year-old with limited experience. You looked at me with spiritual eyes—much like Samuel when he bypassed all David's brothers to find the one who, by human standards, was the least qualified. I wouldn't be where I am today if it weren't for your solid support, willingness to take time with me, and passion about leading our church into a genuine lifestyle of encountering the true God.

All my friends and family—thank you for your consistent support and knack for keeping me humble and down-to-earth. It is so great to have you in my life. I wish I could single all of you out by name. Thankfully, your names are already written in a far more important book, and that's the one that counts. Keep spreading the Kingdom.

endorsements

Art Thomas' book, *The Word of Knowledge in Action*, speaks of a lifestyle that is both practical and powerful—and ultimately available to every believer. He shares wonderful personal stories and insights that help to create great hunger in readers. These stories connect readers with their own ability to hear and activate them to walk in this gift in everyday experiences. *The Word of Knowledge in Action* is a timely book, as God is releasing His Church in a fresh and powerful way of bringing people into an experience with God.

Bill Johnson
Senior Pastor of Bethel Church in Redding, California
Author of *When Heaven Invades Earth* and
Face to Face with God

The Word of Knowledge in Action is a great book. Would that all pastors and their flocks would study it and live its message. Art Thomas is right when he says that if more Christians would seek the Lord for the gift of words of knowledge, and learn to apply them appropriately, that would vivify the Church and make words of knowledge powerful everyday tools for evangelism, for healing, and for the enhancement of nearly every other gift of the Holy Spirit.

Thomas imparts much needed wisdom and caution to a Church grown leery by wild and irresponsible applications of many spiritual gifts. Most appealing is that he centers on reception, use, and results of words of knowledge in the love and courtesy of our Lord Jesus Christ. I urge readers to purchase the book and let its words concerning words of knowledge seep into every other aspect of Christian living and ministry.

John Loren Sandford
Founder, Elijah House Ministries, Inc.
Author, *The Elijah Task, Elijah Among Us,* and
Healing the Wounded Spirit

We live in an age when more and more Christians have not only abandoned the essentials of the faith for doctrines of demons, but a time when supposedly spiritual practices and assumptions are increasingly based on experience rather than on the solid revelation of the Word of God. The result is a subtle—or not so subtle—drift that results in shipwreck of the faith, foolishness in ministry, and an erosion of creditability for those of us who do not share the foolishness.

Art Thomas' book is a solid, sane, and biblical exposition of the nature of the word of knowledge—a gift much misunderstood and most often interpreted through the filter of experience. The reader can trust what he writes. More significantly, Art has connected with the heart of the Father. I highly recommend this book!"

R. Loren Sandford
Senior Pastor of New Song Fellowship
Author, *Purifying the Prophetic, Understanding Prophetic People,*
and *The Prophetic Church*

There are many books to be found on spiritual gifts—and I've read my share—whose emphases tend to gravitate toward the individual distinctions of the gifts and how they are respectively applied. Art Thomas presents an insightful examination of the Word of Knowledge found throughout the Word of God. He responsibly demonstrates the unmistakable interrelationship between this and other spiritual gifts, as well as its companion support of various aspects of ministry including healing, deliverance, intercession, and evangelism.

Art brings a fresh contribution to the conversation on spiritual gifts and their integral function in everyday life. Many captivating stories underscore how the Word of Knowledge is active, even as they complement the Biblical examples found throughout the book. Assimilating its content will compel the reader to pursue the gifts of the Spirit with invigorated enthusiasm.

Quinn Schipper
Founder and President of OIKOS Network Ministries, Inc.
Author, *The Language of Forgiveness* and *Trading Faces*

Subjective interpretation of the prophetic has become prob-
lematic in the Charismatic church. God's Word is never
subjective, but supernaturally objective toward setting captives free. Being the voice of revelation to a world in need of
Him is an honor and a responsibility for ambassadors called
by His name.

Art Thomas takes us on a journey toward plumb-line
truth in the relevant and timely releasing of Father's "Words
of Knowledge." There is no greater teacher than experience;
and through biblically aligned experience, Art delivers a tre-
mendous work that both teaches and empowers.

Robert Ricciardelli
Founder of Converging Zone Network and
Visionary Advancement Strategies

Christ only did what He saw the Father doing, and confessed
that when He stepped outside of what the Father was doing,
He was able to do nothing (see John 5:19). This is quite a statement coming from God Himself, walking the earth as a man.
How did Christ know what the Father was doing, that He may
be able to drastically change every situation working contrary
to God's will? He supernaturally functioned in the Word of
Knowledge via an intimate relationship with the Father. Without this majestic gift from above, we can be assured that Jesus
would have worked far fewer miracles than He did. Surely it is
of utmost importance for us to learn how to walk in this reality
if Christ, God Himself, could do nothing outside of it.

Art does a wonderful job at explaining this imperative in
The Word of Knowledge in Action. Mystical realities that have

confused and confounded some in the past are communicated with a simplicity that causes the reader to think, "Wait a second, I can do this!" If you want some fresh revelation that empowers you to live a supernatural lifestyle and walk as Christ walked, consume the words on the pages of this book like a starved man eats bread.

Tyler Johnson
Founder of the Dead-Raising Teams
Author, *Stories of the Supernatural*

Art Thomas is not first of all a writer looking for his niche in the Christian book world. He is the "real deal" with a genuine heart to reach unconvinced people and help the convinced reach them as well. What better way to catch the attention of someone than to "read a piece of their mail" that only Jesus could have known about and cared to reveal!

Art's book is filled with real-life accounts and counsel that he has practiced and helped many people step into. Art is a personal friend and co-worker, but his best friend is Jesus, who he wants everybody to know. Read the book, step into it, and you can do "even greater things" just as Jesus promised.

Dan Vander Velde
Senior Pastor of Fowlerville Freedom Center, A/G
Fowlerville, Michigan

This book, *The Word of Knowledge in Action*, should cause us as true believers to rekindle our need for the operation of the Spirit. The Spirit of God has many gifts he longs to pour through our personal lives. I feel that Art encourages and prompts us, in our walk with God, to crave the Spirit and action of the gifts—especially to function in the Word of Knowledge, which has not been given much attention in this generation.

As I read the book, I reminisced over the Old and New Testament passages. I was moved by how many times God has worked through the Word of Knowledge throughout history. God has not changed. God desires, more than we could ever imagine, to utilize His people in this day to reveal His knowledge so that He can accomplish His will.

Also, the extraordinary personal testimonies that Art shares will stir your heart so that you long to experience God's Spirit working in your personal world. This Word of Knowledge, as I have individually experienced, is much needed for a world that is lost and disillusioned. People need to recognize that God knows them and He values them. I trust you will read this book and allow the Spirit to make use of your life.

Brooks T. McElhenny
Senior Pastor of Northville Christian
Northville, Michigan

contents

Foreword 19

Preface 25

Introduction 33

Chapter 1
Clearly Defining the Word of Knowledge 37

Chapter 2
The Word of Knowledge and Prophecy 53

Chapter 3
The Word of Knowledge and Visions and Dreams . . . 69

Chapter 4
The Word of Knowledge and Physical Healing 93

Chapter 5
The Word of Knowledge and Intercession 107

Chapter 6
The Word of Knowledge and Evangelism.......... 119

Chapter 7
The Word of Knowledge At Work in Ministry 139

Chapter 8
Pitfalls to Avoid 159

Chapter 9
Activating and Cultivating the Word
of Knowledge................................... 175

Conclusion 187

foreword ↗

At last, an entire book teaching us what the gift of a word of knowledge really is—and in a balanced, thoroughly biblical, and theologically accurate way.

When I was filled with the Holy Spirit in 1958, few in old-line churches had received the Lord, much less having been filled with His Holy Spirit. It seemed nobody knew anything. The spiritual landscape was barren. We had to stumble into everything we now know by trial and error, repenting and trying again.

Since then, in only a little over fifty years, the Lord has resurrected the sleeping giant of the Church (as in Ezek. 37:1-10); and the waters of revelation that were then only a trickle have risen until it's wading and swimming time in order to keep up with the flow of what God is doing (see Ezek. 47:5). It is amazing how many varied, wise, and knowledgeable ministries God has raised up and what a multitude of books have come pouring out on nearly every topic since that time. But over the years, in all those essays, what has been missing (at least to my knowledge) is that none yet has written something well done and sensible specifically on the subject of the Word of Knowledge. Therefore, readers will find in Art Thomas' book, *The Word of Knowledge in Action*, a great blessing. This book fills a gap in how to understand and employ this very wonderful spiritual gift.

Art Thomas begins with a concise and clear definition of what the gift of a Word of Knowledge really is—a momentary revelation of what is on the mind of our Lord Jesus Christ. Words of Knowledge are simply the Holy Spirit revealing to us the thoughts of Christ that He wants us to know in any situation. The word is "momentary" because ordinarily, Words of Knowledge are not about the sweep of history but simply whatever is happening and needful to know in that given moment.

This definition removes the gift from our own possibly psychic strivings and places words of revelation solely within the present will of God. It makes clear that true Words of Knowledge are His enterprise, solely for His purposes. They are given by Him—not enacted by our own natural abilities. To me this comes as a breath of fresh air and a mighty relief since I have wrestled many times with the sad fruits of supposed words from Christians trying to serve God but being caught up in their own often fleshly strivings. Words of Knowledge ought to emanate from Christians at rest in the love of God for them and proceed through them to others. Thomas rightly insists that Words of Knowledge are our Lord's love, expressed through Christians who can hear and will respond.

He states again and again that it is one thing to receive a Word of Knowledge and another to know what to do with it. Being ourselves pioneers in the prophetic gift, Paula and

I have had to regularly teach that if you receive something from God, that's only part of the task. The greater responsibility is now on you to find out what to do with whatever He has given. Should you say it, remain still and ponder, or respond with intercession? How, when, and in what circumstance should you present what God has given? Art addresses these questions and more, carefully teaching how and when Words of Knowledge can be given in helpful rather than harmful ways. How valuable that is!

Much of the teaching is delightfully conveyed by stories and testimonies. Teachings in logical words come mainly through our left brain and do some good; but when stories and testimonies come, they move through the right brain into the heart, bringing healing or whatever good the Lord intends. Readers will find themselves quickened in faith and emboldened to risk trying their wings (and gently convicted by the question, "Why haven't I been doing this enough myself?").

Some have made the mistake of demanding that prophetic words and Words of Knowledge be expressed succinctly and with word-for-word accuracy, otherwise being considered false words. These critics have not understood the way of our Lord. The Holy Spirit can speak directly, succinctly, and accurately; but I think most often He chooses to speak through parables or by "dark speech." Psalm 78:2 says, "*I will open my mouth in a parable, I will utter dark sayings of old*" (NKJV). There came a time when Jesus refused to teach except by parables. Why "dark speech?" Why not clearly? For many reasons, but perhaps the most important is that He wants us to ponder. In the meditating, we will be drawn closer to Him, which is what He wants. Having to puzzle quickens our realization that Kingdom-living is purposefully an introduction into mystery, into a world where we can't depend on our own knowledge and practiced ways. We can't quickly and perhaps prematurely say, "I've got it," and so basically say, "I don't need You anymore, Lord; I know what to do." Living with the jagged edges of mystery forces us into dependence on Him. Throughout the book, Art relates stories about how the Lord would give him and/or his team words that meant little or nothing to them, or even seemed irrelevant or nutty, but drove them to our Lord for more clarification. With this clarity, these words became door-openers to hearts and effective ministry. Struggling to comprehend puzzling words causes us to come to know and love our Lord far more than had He simply spoken directly, and that is what it's all about anyway—falling ever more in love with our wonderful Lord.

A most pleasing thing to me about the book is that Art Thomas continually calls for death of self, and locates error where it truly originates—in pride. Readers should pay close attention to the chapter on pitfalls. Being both a teacher and counselor, I can't tell you (being ethically restrained) the woeful stories of so many who could have been saved painful falls if they had only possessed opportunity to let this chapter sink deeply into the heart.

Finally, Art asks how we can receive the gift of a Word of Knowledge. Read the book; he will give you good advice for the searching. But I want to close this foreword by saying that first and above all you must let our Lord fill you with His love for people and His passion to heal and set lives straight. Paula and I filled seventeen books with keys of knowledge for ministry, all of which came as Words of Knowledge in the act of ministry. While ministering to someone, we would come up against blockages and things we couldn't understand or know how to minister to. So we would cry out our usual fervent, intellectual, and righteous prayer: "Help!" Then, in the context of ministry, where need prompted humility, our Lord would give the revelations that became the books. We never got a Word of Knowledge just because we wanted to know more than we did. For us, Words of Knowledge always came as expressions of our Lord's love in ministry to His loved ones, when desperation called from our hearts to His. Therefore I say, if you desire the gift of a Word of Knowledge, don't seek it by itself first or only; seek to minister His love to others, and when you need it, He will pour His revelations into your mind and heart.

Let *The Word of Knowledge in Action* become your springboard into more effective ministry, and into the joy of knowing and loving our Lord Jesus more and more when you are truly given into letting Him express His love for others.

John Loren Sandford
Founder, Elijah House Ministries, Inc.

preface ↗

I think I was born in a pew. There was never a time in my life when I wasn't actively involved in a church setting. I've done everything from traditional church, to church planting, to a house church. I've swung the pendulum from the extremes of organization to spontaneity and back again (hoping to eventually wind up somewhere in the middle). The forms may have changed, but it was always church, and it was always enwrapped in Pentecostal heritage.

I grew up in a family that regularly talked about the Holy Spirit, hearing God's voice, and sharing testimonies of God's supernatural involvement in human lives. I saw examples of dedicated, conversational prayer in the lives of my parents and grandmother. From a very young age, a hunger for the supernatural was birthed in my soul. God placed me in just the right family environment to prepare me for what He has called me to do.

With that said, my life isn't a fairy tale. While it is true that I was baptized in water at the age of 8 and filled with the Holy Spirit at the age of 11, I don't think I had a true revelation of God until I was almost 20. It came when the Holy

Spirit dramatically set me free from a seven-year addiction to pornography—a story that may one day need to be a book in itself. What matters in context here is that I went from "knowing all the answers" about God to actually knowing Christ and the power of His resurrection.

When that shift took place in my heart, I got downright radical. I pored over the Scriptures and spent all my free time in prayer and worship. I was passionate and genuine in my love for God, but He still had a lot of work to do in me to break me of my self-life. Several different people prophesied over me (at different times) that God had called me to teach with wisdom beyond my years, prophesy, work miracles, and heal the sick. That's a word everyone wants, but I can tell you from experience that it blinded me with pride. I was hungry for it to happen, but I had not yet had a deep, inner revelation of the cross to really do the job.

Without the humility to bear the ministry that was promised, I found myself lacking fulfillment. God granted me little glimpses of what would come, but His Word is true that He opposes the proud!

Not realizing that my lack of spiritual gifts was a matter of my pride, I decided to take matters into my own hands. I started reading every Charismatic book I could get my hands on. I began with anything I could find that contained the words "prophet," "prophecy," or "spiritual gifts." Then I read everything I could find about physical healing and deliverance. But all these books only served to feed my pride and strengthen my resolve to really make something of myself. As Paul said in First Corinthians 8:1, *"Knowledge puffs up, but love builds up."*

Thankfully, God placed key people into my life who helped bring me out of that mess. Rather than trying to fix me with more knowledge, they chose to build me up in love. I started to see my self-life getting dismantled as Jesus became more and more evident. It wouldn't be right for me to start this book without acknowledging some of those who loved me to life.

I met my wife, Robin, when she was 15 and I was 17. She is the first and only girl I ever dated, and we took our time letting our relationship blossom. It sounds beautiful, but our first few years together were anything but. She was great, but I was a mess. Robin walked beside me throughout my entire battle with the inner kingdom I had built out of pride. She faithfully stood by my side and fought for my deliverance from evil spirits that I had allowed access. She even graciously walked with me through the transition during which I finally stepped up to lead as the spiritual head of our relationship. We dated for seven years, were married June 7, 2009, and now have the greatest, most God-honoring relationship I can imagine. Robin's character is above reproach, and our love for each other is an example of Christ and His Bride, the Church. Her spiritual gifts of healing, hospitality, and encouragement have become a key component of our ministry together. I couldn't be happier to share my life with her. Thank you, Robin, for being the greatest wife I could ever imagine.

Two other key players were my parents, Gaylord and Linda Thomas. Not only did they raise me well, but I honestly felt as though their worlds revolved around me. They gave me a childhood rich with experience and opportunities for spiritual growth, and their daily prayers have been instrumental in the transformation God has brought into my life. Mom and Dad still live exemplary lives of faith and passion for Christ. You can't spend more than a half hour with them without hearing a testimony of something God has done in them or through them.

Then there was my grandmother, Pearl Thomas, who has shaped my understanding of prayer more than anyone else in this world. When my grandpa passed away, she said, "Well, Lord, it's just You and me now, so You're going to have to be everything Bud was and more." I never met my grandpa, but I sure did meet Jesus. I can remember Grandma cooking dinner and carrying on a conversation with Jesus as if He were cutting the carrots right next to her. Grandma was always positive, full of faith, and kind to everyone—a true representation of a Christ-like life. I know I would not be who I am today without her love and example.

There have also been many pastors who regularly spent personal time with me and my family: Greg Gentry, Paul Spear, Dan Strength, John Harris, Otis Buchan, Mike Byrum, Brandon Hukill, Dan Vander Velde, Shane Fritz, Brooks McElhenny, Jason Elston, Matt South, and Scott Laurain (to name a few). Three of these especially stand out in the shaping of my life.

The first is Dan Vander Velde, who believed in me when it seemed no one else did. He met me when I was still very much entrenched in my pride and addictions. I had all manner of crazy ideas about church, Christianity, and matters of the spiritual realm. I was constantly striving for acceptance, which isn't healthy for a person who wants spiritual gifts. Nevertheless, Pastor Dan embraced me as a brother, paced with me, and was perhaps the most instrumental tool in God's belt during the time of turn-around in my life. Pastor Dan walked me through my most challenging vices. With his counsel and the application of the cross of Christ, I discovered a newfound ability to relate to people, practice spiritual gifts with greater freedom, escape from the need to perform, and genuinely sense the love of my Father in Heaven. Pastor Dan is an encourager like none other, and I wish everyone in the world could spend even one year being impacted by his ministry. I was blessed to spend nearly five.

The second is Shane Fritz. Pastor Shane and I became fast friends and would regularly meet together to share testimonies of God's power and salvation in our ministries. Not only did Shane help shape my perspective of the supernatural, but he also welcomed me into it. We loved to minister alongside each other to bring people freedom, deliverance, healing, and wholeness in Christ. As much as we spoke into each other's lives, Shane truly discipled me like no one else ever has. During my most formative years in ministry, Shane would meet with me almost every week to share a meal and talk about what God was doing in my life. He would challenge me to live above the status quo and remain passionate for Christ. He breathed vision into my life and challenged me to discover God's vision for myself. Shane is a man who lives a naturally supernatural lifestyle, and I'm so grateful that God placed him in my life to show me how to do the same.

Third is Jason Elston. Pastor Jason and I built our friendship while working alongside each other at Northville Christian Assembly. In an organizational sense, he is my boss; but in a relational sense, he is the most prominent voice in my life at this time regarding the things of God. He has stretched me to do things I never thought were possible in my life. He has trained me to be focused and organized—something I still haven't perfected, but something every teacher and pastor in my history has tried to do without much headway. Jason is the type of friend with whom I can share any struggle, and he is always ready with Spirit-filled wisdom, counsel, and prayer.

I would also go so far as to give significant credit to the various authors who have played a role in shaping my theology and relationship with God. Some, like Watchman Nee, Andrew Murray, and Smith Wigglesworth, have long since gone to be with Jesus. Then there are the more contemporary writers like Bill Johnson, Kris Vallotton, John and Paula Sandford, R. Loren Sandford, and Paul Hattaway—some of whom may yet have more writings to share. I have only met a few of these people, and yet I feel as though I have spent hours, days, and even months learning at each one's feet as I have read and studied their works, putting them into practice with passion for Christ.

Every one of these people (and many more) has been used by God to help bring me to the place where I am today. I can't even begin to list all the other teachers, family members, church leaders, friends, and students who have also played key roles. My point is simply to show that I can't take any glory for myself. Anything of value that I bring to you in this book is either directly or indirectly from God.

I pray that I can become one of these people to you. I hope your faith, theology, and passion for Jesus Christ are impacted and strengthened as you read this book. I desire that as you learn, your spirit will grow more than your intellect. May God genuinely bless your spiritual life as you discover the intricacies of the spiritual gift known as the Word of Knowledge.

introduction ↗

I closed the book in frustration. It was the fifth book I had read about spiritual gifts, and it was the fifth unique definition for the Word of Knowledge. I found the inconsistency utterly obnoxious.

I'm the type of person who likes to learn things. I'm also the type of person who hates to waste my time learning things that aren't true. So when five different authors contradict each other in whole or in part, it bothers me!

In desperation for something solid, I grabbed the giant *Strong's Concordance* from my mother's bookshelf and started looking for any references I could find about the Word of Knowledge. I found just one:

> *But the manifestation of the Spirit is given to each one for the profit of all: for to one is given the word of wisdom through the Spirit, to another the word of knowledge through the same Spirit...* (1 Corinthians 12:7-8 NKJV).

That was no help at all! All it tells us is that the Word of Knowledge exists, that the Holy Spirit gives it, and that it ranks among the other spiritual gifts listed in that chapter.

Naturally, the cynical side of me jumped into high gear. What basis did all these other authors have for the definitions they brought to the table? What right did they have to define something without any biblical grounds for their definition?

As much as I'm passionate about the supernatural power of God and the reality of the spiritual realm, I'm a stickler for sound doctrine. The word "doctrine" has gotten a bad rap in many Charismatic circles. The problem stems from a kneejerk reaction that some have had to religious people who were sold-out on wrong doctrine. Naturally, when you truly believe wrong doctrine, you treat it like right doctrine, which in turn gives the word "doctrine" a bad name.

Suppose we applied this mindset to Rolex watches. Everybody agrees that Rolex is one of the most recognized names in the watch industry, known for their quality, value, and precision. Nevertheless, nearly anyone who has been to the inner city has seen a fake Rolex being passed off as the real deal. Now I ask you: Just because there is such a thing as a fake Rolex, should we decide that all watches bearing the Rolex name are fake? Should we define this brand name by the imitations or by the genuine articles? Doctrine is the same way. Just because false doctrine exists doesn't mean all doctrine is bad.

I consider doctrine to be very spiritual. In fact, I believe the Holy Spirit is presently bringing a revival of doctrine to the church—helping us to provide solid biblical grounds for everything we believe. Gone are the days when Christians were content to base their beliefs on subjective experience or philosophical human reasoning. All experience and philosophy must bow to God's truth.

For several years, I purposefully decided not to buy into any definition of the Word of Knowledge. If it wasn't spelled out in the Bible, I didn't see any reason to put any confidence in the thoughts and opinions of others. I believed that it happens in the Church today because the Holy Spirit is alive today, but I accepted that since we can't define it, we can't identify it.

It was within this frame of mind that the Lord showed me something in the Scriptures that I had never seen before. Suddenly, the Word of Knowledge took on new meaning. The definition jumped right off the page. I saw how it could function powerfully in the church. I saw how it was integrated into the Body of Christ. I saw how it could work hand-in-hand with prophecy, visions, dreams, healing, intercession, evangelism, and various other forms of ministry. Most importantly, I saw the biblical evidence for all of it.

This book is the fruit of that revelation. Through personal experience, supported by biblical examples and doctrinal truth, I'm going to introduce you to a spiritual gift that has flown under the radar in the Church for years. Sure, we've captured glimpses of what this gift might mean, but for the most part, we've only scraped the tip of the iceberg. In the following pages, not only will you learn various functions and uses for this spiritual gift, but you will discover how to activate it, enhance it, and implement it with focus and wisdom. Get ready to discover what it really is to receive a Word of Knowledge and use it for the glory of God.

Chapter 1

clearly defining
the word of knowledge ↗

The Word of Knowledge is perhaps one of the most misunderstood gifts of the Spirit. It is mentioned by name only once in the entire Bible, and that one mention barely even hints at the definition:

> *But the manifestation of the Spirit is given to each one for the profit of all: for to one is given the word of wisdom through the Spirit, to another the word of knowledge through the same Spirit...* (1 Corinthians 12:7-8 NKJV).

I have heard many preachers define the Word of Knowledge based on personal experience, but few have used the entirety of Scripture to back up their ideas. I once sat through an hour-long teaching about how the Word of Knowledge relates to physical healing without the teacher once mentioning that its definition could possibly go deeper. Additionally, Smith Wigglesworth—whose biography and old sermons were very foundational in my life—took the stance that the Word of Knowledge merely has to do with preaching divine revelation born out of reading the Bible.[1] Still others have claimed that this gift has to do with a person's ability to learn facts and information. These vast differences among definitions raise one big obvious question: Who's right?

With all due respect to these many authors and teachers, I have yet to hear someone present a full picture based on Scripture. The variance in definitions, I believe, is likely because they are born out of personal experience. Yes, experience is important—if all we had was a doctrine with no experience, I would question the validity of it. But experience apart from the correlation of Scripture is not solid ground to stand on.

I'm the type of person who is completely comfortable with the idea that some things are just mysteries. I like a mysterious God. But Paul wrote about the Word of Knowledge as though it was incredibly commonplace. After all, why write a definition if everyone in your audience knows what you're talking about? And if this spiritual gift was supposed to be such a natural part of the Church, surely it's not meant to be one of those "mysteries" that God wants to keep hidden!

As happens in many discoveries, I simply stumbled across the answer. As I was reading the Gospel of John, I came to a place where Jesus was talking about the Holy Spirit and how He operates. I realized that this was a glimpse into the definition of every single spiritual gift—and therefore, to my delight, the Word of Knowledge:

> [Jesus said,] "I have much more to say to you, more than you can now bear. But when he, the Spirit of truth, comes, he will guide you into all truth. He will not speak on his

own; he will speak only what he hears, and he will tell you what is yet to come. He will bring glory to me by taking from what is mine and making it known to you. All that belongs to the Father is mine. That is why I said the Spirit will take from what is mine and make it known to you (John 16:12-15).

The Holy Spirit takes from what is Christ's and makes it known to us. That's how He works. So the gift of faith, for instance, is not simply the Holy Spirit stirring up our limited human faith. Rather, it is a moment when the Holy Spirit makes Jesus' faith known to us! Jesus currently sits at His Father's right hand, hears Him in person, and sees Him face to face—who could possibly have more faith than the Son of God? Imagine the ramifications of His Holy Spirit taking that very same faith from Jesus and making it known to a human being on earth! Now, that's a gift of faith! The same goes for every other spiritual gift.

Given what Jesus told us about how the Holy Spirit operates, we have a very clear insight into the full definition of the Word of Knowledge. In short, the Word of Knowledge is not simply the Holy Spirit giving you the ability to know things you otherwise wouldn't know. Rather, this gift takes place when the Holy Spirit takes something Jesus knows and reveals it to us.

All of a sudden, the definition opens up to a whole world of possibilities! Maybe it's something Jesus knows about His Word, the Bible. Maybe it's something He knows about a person for whom you're praying. Maybe it's something He knows about things people have been doing in secret that need to be addressed. Maybe it's something He knows about a person's physical condition. The list goes on and on.

There are also variances in the ways this gift is experienced. Some suddenly feel that they know something, which moments before would have never crossed their mind. Some may suddenly grasp a whole concept in Scripture as they read the Word of God. Still others have physical sensations in their bodies. Others experience this gift through visions and dreams. All these are ways the same Holy Spirit takes something Jesus knows and reveals it to His Church.

The Word of Knowledge is not Natural Knowledge

One easy mistake to make is to assume that the Word of Knowledge is somehow on the same level as mere human knowledge. Some have even gone so far as to misquote Scripture by teaching about a "gift of knowledge." I've heard it said in some circles that this gift is demonstrated by intelligent, scholarly people in the Church. It's not uncommon to see this gift presented in this way on the many spiritual gift assessment tests circulating throughout Christendom today.

A Word of Knowledge, though, is different. It doesn't have anything to do with accumulated, natural knowledge developed over time. In the case of this spiritual gift, a person is actually imparted a nugget of Jesus' own knowledge. It's just a piece. The New International Version translates the

Greek to say "Message of Knowledge." It's just that—a message. It's like getting mail. Opening a letter from someone doesn't cause you to instantly understand that person's entire life story. On the contrary, it gives you a glimpse into the specific subject the person wrote about. The Word of Knowledge is just as specific.

The Gift of Knowledge and Understanding

By and large, the ability to accumulate knowledge is merely one of those natural abilities God grants to all people, in varying capacities. The gifts of the Spirit, on the other hand, are distributed throughout the Church. Some of us have one gift, and some of us have another.

> *There are different kinds of gifts, but the same Spirit. There are different kinds of service, but the same Lord. There are different kinds of working, but the same God works all of them in all men.... All these are the work of one and the same Spirit, and he gives them to each one, just as he determines* (1 Corinthians 12:4-6, 11).

If natural knowledge were a spiritual gift, that would mean many people in the Church (and even fewer outside the Church) could not learn anything at all.

However, there is another spiritual gift that does affect natural knowledge and is easily confused with the Word of Knowledge. In the book of Daniel, we learn that there is a special gift from God called "Knowledge and Understanding."

King Nebuchadnezzar took over Jerusalem and carried into exile some of the Israelites from the nobility and the royal families. Among them were Daniel and his three friends, best known by their Babylonian names of Shadrach, Meshach, and Abednego.

It's at this early point in the story that we first hear about this spiritual gift:

> *To these four young men God gave knowledge and understanding of all kinds of literature and learning...* (Daniel 1:17a).

This passage is clear that the knowledge and understanding the four young Hebrews had was "given" to them by God. That makes it a gift. And in their case, this gift had to do with "all kinds of literature and learning."

So the question naturally arises as to whether or not this was the same thing as the Word of Knowledge Paul talked about. I believe I can say with certainty that it's a different gift.

When Jesus walked this earth, he occasionally demonstrated the gift of a Word of Knowledge as the Holy Spirit supernaturally revealed something to Him that only His Father could have known—we'll see several examples of this later. But He also demonstrated a gift of Knowledge and Understanding, just like Daniel and his three friends.

It feels weird for some of us to think this way, but Jesus—though He was the Son of God—also had to learn. He didn't pop out of the womb preaching sermons in eloquent

Aramaic! Rather, He went through the process of development just like the rest of us. (See Luke 2:46-47; Luke 2:51-52; and Hebrews 5:8-9.)

In Luke's Gospel, we can see the gift of Knowledge and Understanding at work in Jesus. His family went to Jerusalem for the annual Passover feast. On their return trip, after a full day of travel, Joseph and Mary suddenly realized that Jesus wasn't with the caravan! They raced back to Jerusalem to find Him.

After three days they found him in the temple courts, sitting among the teachers, listening to them and asking them questions. Everyone who heard him was amazed at his understanding and his answers (Luke 2:46-47).

Jesus amazed the crowds with his understanding. That means He wasn't merely learning like any other twelve-year-old boy. Rather, He was demonstrating a capacity for knowledge and understanding that seemed, perhaps, supernatural in nature. This was a gift of Knowledge and Understanding just like the four Hebrew captives demonstrated in the book of Daniel.

Today, Jesus is no longer a humble servant walking the earth. Father God has exalted Him to the highest place of authority in Heaven and on earth. His name is exalted above every name! He is King of kings and Lord of lords! This means that He no longer needs to learn. Colossians 2:3 says that *"in Christ are hidden all the treasures of wisdom and knowledge."* In other words, Jesus now knows everything there is to know.

Nothing in all creation is hidden from Him. He knows the contents of every book that has ever been written. He even knows the hearts and intentions of the authors. For this reason, I have to believe that this spiritual gift should somehow have an even more dynamic manifestation today!

For Daniel and his three friends to have been given "knowledge and understanding of all kinds of literature and learning," it only makes sense that the Holy Spirit took from Christ's capacity for knowledge and understanding and made it known to them.[2] They partook in a supernatural ability to learn like Jesus.

The Word of Knowledge is a momentary revelation of certain facts in the mind of Christ. In contrast, the gift of Knowledge and Understanding is more of an ability or life-skill belonging to Jesus. It's not momentary, and it's not just one little chunk of information. On the contrary, it's what happens when the Holy Spirit enables a believer to learn and understand just like Jesus did.

The Original Language

In America, we hear the word "knowledge" and think of mere facts. The contestant who wins several weeks in a row on *Jeopardy* is clearly the one with the most knowledge, right? That may be how our culture understands the word, but that's not what was intended when Paul wrote First Corinthians 12.

For the Greeks, to have knowledge of something was to have certainty based on experience or personal interaction.

For instance, to have knowledge of Christ didn't mean merely knowing facts about Him; rather it meant that you enjoy a relationship with Him. In fact, Paul hailed from the Hebrew culture, where the word "know" implied deep intimacy. Consider Genesis 4:1, which says in the King James Version, "... *Adam knew Eve his wife; and she conceived...*" Clearly, "knowing" was a matter of being intimately acquainted.

So Paul—a self-proclaimed "Hebrew of Hebrews"— wrote to the Greeks with a very healthy understanding of the word "knowledge." He wasn't talking about the Holy Spirit revealing trivia. Rather, we're dealing with Christ's intimate involvement in the world. As the old song goes, "Jesus knows all about our troubles." He "knows" because He himself suffered in every way we ever will.

He was despised and rejected by men, a man of sorrows, and familiar with suffering. Like one from whom men hide their faces he was despised, and we esteemed him not (Isaiah 53:3).

For we do not have a high priest who is unable to sympathize with our weaknesses, but we have one who has been tempted in every way, just as we are—yet was without sin (Hebrews 4:15).

So when someone says Jesus knows what's going on in your life, it's not simply that He's aware. He truly knows. He's been there, and He struggles right alongside you.

This affects our definition of the Word of Knowledge because it means we're not just getting "information" from Jesus, but we're also getting the heart to go with it.

Getting the Heart

I once taught a class to a group of men and women who were about to serve as staff at a camp for foster children. The session was about letting God heal the hurts in our own lives so that we're more effective at soothing the hurts in the lives of others.

I really only spoke for about twenty minutes—describing the biblical work of sanctification and inner transformation. Then I opened the floor for questions before stepping into a time of practical application and ministry.

One woman raised her hand right away. I quickly found out she didn't really have a question. Rather, she must have been so stirred by the teaching that she couldn't wait any longer for the ministry time.

"I was hurt at a church. The pastor said some harsh things about me, and the whole congregation turned on me. I just don't know if I can really forgive them and trust another church!" she said.

Up until this point, I had never really experienced a Word of Knowledge. God had used me to prophesy, speak in tongues, and interpret tongues; but the Word of Knowledge was something about which I had only read. Nevertheless, while this woman spoke, a strange thing happened.

As she briefly mentioned that church, I suddenly had absolute certainty that she was in the right. She truly didn't deserve the treatment she had received at that church.

To be honest, my logical brain was saying, "She probably deserved it—there's no way a pastor and an entire church would do this without justification." But there persisted a strong conviction in my heart that she just wasn't at fault and didn't need to carry the guilt of what had happened to her.

So when she finished, I replied, "It wasn't your fault."

That was it. I didn't go into some great detail; I simply said it wasn't her fault. But this wasn't enough.

"Others have said that before, but how can I know it's true?" she asked, genuinely seeking an inspired reply.

Suddenly, I was certain of something else. I responded, "Because this didn't just happen to you at that one church. I have the feeling it happened to you at three different churches. Is that true?"

Tears welled up in the woman's eyes as she slowly nodded yes.

I then said, "Jesus was there at all three churches, and He knows it wasn't your fault."

The woman sobbed. I placed my hand on her shoulder and prayed for her. Those sitting around her prayed too. In one instant, God dramatically set that woman free from years of hurt, and the tool He used was the Word of Knowledge.

It wasn't that I simply had facts—the information came with conviction and a gut feeling that "this just isn't right!" My emotions were stirred as if I had watched the entire scene myself. Jesus knew all about her situation, and the Holy Spirit took that knowledge and made it known to me.

Simply Knowing

It didn't take a voice from Heaven, a vision, a dream, an angelic visitation, or anything else. I just somehow knew. I had never met this woman before that day—nor had I ever heard anything about her—but I simply knew what had transpired in her life. This happened not because I'm anything special. It's simply because Jesus had been there in her circumstance, and the Holy Spirit let me experience what Jesus knew. As a result, I simply knew.

This is the most foundational form of this gift. It's not the result of reading the Bible or seeking revelation in a time of prayer. It's simply the sudden realization that you truly know something that you couldn't possibly know apart from spiritual intervention.

Jesus practiced this as well. In Luke 11, Jesus cast a demon out of a man. The man had been unable to talk; but when Jesus commanded the evil spirit to leave, the man spoke! This shocked the crowd, and they began to wonder if Jesus was using the power of the devil to drive out demons.

Then comes verse 17, in which we see one quick statement: "*Jesus knew their thoughts*...." That's right! Jesus knew the thoughts of the crowd! I think that's pretty cool since we're not speaking about knowing one individual's thoughts but rather the thoughts of an entire crowd! This came by revelation of the Holy Spirit.

For who among men knows the thoughts of a man except the man's spirit within him?... (1 Corinthians 2:11a).

When Jesus walked this planet, He did so as a man rather than as God. Paul said that He gave up everything about Himself that could be considered "God" and humbled Himself all the way to the point of death on a cross.[3] In other words, Jesus "the man" didn't have the capacity to know men's thoughts on His own. "For who among men knows the thoughts of a man...?"

Jesus needed to rely on His Father in Heaven who *"knows the secrets of the heart"* (Ps. 44:21). He had Words of Knowledge by which the Holy Spirit made known what the Father knows.

Some might say that this affects our definition, but remember the passage from John 16 in which Jesus talked about the Holy Spirit. Pay attention to verse 15, in which Jesus said, *"All that belongs to the Father is mine. That is why I said the Spirit will take from what is mine and make it known to you."* In other words, all knowledge—both natural and supernatural—and all spiritual gifts originate with the Father. (See James 1:17.)

When Jesus walked this earth, He received Words of Knowledge when the Holy Spirit took what the Father knew and made it known to Him. But today, the Father has glorified His Son and delights to let Jesus be the source of everything for the Church. So He joyfully lets Jesus receive the credit for the Church's success.

Simplifying the Definition

In short, the gift of a Word of Knowledge takes place when the Holy Spirit takes from Christ's knowledge and makes it known to you. It is not the natural knowledge that we all accumulate throughout life, and it is not the supernatural ability to learn like Jesus. It is also not a strange ability to know all things. It is very simply a glimpse into the mind of Christ by which we share in His "knowing" about a specific incident, thought, or intention.

The following chapters will help unfold this biblical understanding with examples from Scripture, testimonies, and personal experiences to help you understand, embrace, and hopefully, to activate this spiritual gift. Like we saw in the ancient church of Corinth to whom Paul wrote, I believe it's time to re-kindle the normalcy of the Word of Knowledge in today's Church!

Summary Questions

1. Based on Jesus' words that the Holy Spirit will "take from what is Mine and make it known to you," how could we define Spiritual Gifts in general?

_____

_____

2. In what ways do the Greek and Hebrew definitions of "know" differ from our current English understanding of that word?

_____

_____

3. List some categories of things that Jesus knows that would otherwise be unknowable by you.

_____

_____

4. In the next chapter, we will talk about how the Word of Knowledge interacts with the gift of Prophecy. Before you read it, can you think of any ways the two gifts might relate?

_____

_____

Endnotes

1. Smith Wigglesworth (1998). *Smith Wigglesworth on spiritual gifts*. New Kensington, PA: Whitaker House.

2. Yes, I am referring to Old Testament figures receiving from Christ. Many struggle with the idea that Jesus was present in the Old Testament. Entire

books could be written to describe His presence throughout the Hebrew text, so I can only scrape the surface here. For the sake of quick reference, have a look at John 1:1-14; John 17:24; Colossians 1:15; 2 Timothy 1:9; 1 Peter 1:20; 1 John 2:13; Revelation 13:8; and Revelation 22:13.

3. See Philippians 2:5-8. Also notice that in John 5:19, Jesus said, "*...the Son can do nothing by Himself...*"

Chapter 2

the word of knowledge and prophecy ↗

To prophesy is to speak on God's behalf. It's one of the ways God communicates with human beings. The Gift of Prophecy takes place when the Holy Spirit takes the words of Jesus and makes them known by placing them in the heart and mind of a person on earth who speaks them out. Sometimes this is a spontaneous message whereby the speaker doesn't know what he is going to say next until he says it; and at other times it's a prompting in the heart in which the speaker waits for the appropriate time to present the message. Those who practice the Gift of Prophecy are basically the heralds of God—speaking His words audibly when others may not be listening.

This is different from the Word of Knowledge in that prophecy has to do with conveying a message from the voice of Christ whereas the Word of Knowledge has to do with expressing part of the mind of Christ. The Word of Knowledge isn't always easy to put into words at first, whereas the Gift of Prophecy typically comes as words. Additionally, the Word of Knowledge often comes with a sense of ownership, as though you had personally witnessed the event. Prophecy, on the other hand, though it comes with conviction, still has a sense that you're speaking on behalf of another.

Paul said that the purpose of prophecy is to strengthen, encourage, and comfort people. (See 1 Corinthians 14:3.) This may be a message for the moment in which God expresses His love and care for a person, or it may be a message about the future. Either way, God speaks through a man or woman, and the listeners are built up and encouraged.

The Word of Knowledge, however, tends to deal more with information regarding the past and present. Rather than expressing a message, it tends to have more to do with facts surrounding events, thoughts, intentions, actions, ideas, and other such things.

It's important to know how these two gifts differ because it helps us understand how they can be used together. Both gifts are methods by which the Holy Spirit reveals Jesus through the Church, but they're different aspects of Jesus. One has to do with His message, and the other has to do with His knowledge.

Paving the Way for Prophecy

I once had a woman approach me after a church service who said, "Can I ask you to pray for my husband?" Though I had never really known this woman, suddenly the thought "alcohol" popped into my mind. So I simply said that one word.

The woman began to cry and asked, "How did you know?"

At this point, it was clear to me that what she needed most wasn't a teaching on the Word of Knowledge but rather encouragement from God. So I asked the Holy Spirit what Jesus would like to say to her. I then responded with a message from Him, "I feel like God's saying that He has seen your faithfulness in the midst of this trial, and your prayers have not gone unnoticed. He will deliver your husband soon."

I then prayed with her. She also invited a group of us over to her house to pray together. Three months later, the husband quit drinking, moved back to their bedroom from the basement, and started working on patching up their marriage. God opened the woman's heart with a Word of Knowledge, and this made her more receptive to the Gift of Prophecy that followed.

Looking back, I don't believe the prophecy would have been nearly as effective without the Word of Knowledge to break the ice. It was a pretty generic message on its own, and the woman could have easily written it off as the mere words of another well-intentioned Christian. But by my starting with a Word of Knowledge, her attention was captured! She knew that God was speaking, and it stirred her faith.

It's important to note that neither the Word of Knowledge nor the Gift of Prophecy changed this woman's husband. These only served to ignite her faith. Instead, it was that faith and her newfound hope that drove her to passionate prayer with other believers in full trust that God would do what He promised.

Comprehending Prophecy

Prophecy doesn't always have to start with a Word of Knowledge. I've also seen instances where a Word of Knowledge was beneficial afterward.

During the singing one Sunday morning, the Holy Spirit turned my attention toward an older lady in our church and said, "I have given her big spiritual feet. Go tell her."

To be honest, I was a little upset! If God was going to use me to speak His words to someone, why couldn't the message be a normal one? Why couldn't it be something cool? But no—just, "big spiritual feet."

So I walked over to her and said sheepishly, "Hi. I don't know if this means anything to you, but as we were singing, I really felt like the Lord was saying that He has given you big spiritual feet." Then, trying to ignore her attempt at choking back laughter, I asked, "Does that mean anything to you?"

"No, I'm sorry," she answered with a chuckle, "but I'll pray about it!"

Of course—"I'll pray about it"—the default phrase Christians use when they don't want to hurt your feelings with a solid "no."

I walked away saying, "Well, God, I did it. Maybe it wasn't You, but I'm glad I gave it my best shot. If it was You, though, I want to know what You meant so it can be more meaningful to her."

For three days, I prayed about it. To be honest, my primary motivation was mostly that I felt embarrassed! The woman's understanding and spiritual growth were only a secondary reason.

Sure enough, three days later, I left my college between classes to pray at my church, and the Lord finally brought a sudden clear understanding. In an instant, the prophecy made sense as though the message had originally come from my own mind. I understood and knew exactly what God meant.

I sped to the woman's office, and she welcomed me (which I thought was a good sign that she hadn't completely written me off as crazy).

I started by asking, "Hey, I'm just curious if that message I shared with you Sunday ended up meaning anything to you."

"Actually," she replied, "I didn't want to say anything at the time, but I've always felt very self-conscious about how small my feet are. I thought it was interesting that God was saying that, and it was sort of like He was telling me that any of my physical shortcomings would be countered by what He has given me in the spiritual realm. Why? Do you think there's more to it?"

After hearing her reply, I really didn't want to share what I had sensed from the Lord because it was yet another silly thought. But my Word of Knowledge seemed to mesh so well with the interpretation she shared that I couldn't resist.

"Well," I replied, "I was praying about it, and I felt like someone in your company is going to be leaving soon. And when they do, there are many aspects of his portfolio that you're going to need to pick up. When that time comes, you're going to feel like those shoes are too big to fill, but God has given you big spiritual feet to fill this man's shoes."

She laughed again, but I knew this time that she wasn't laughing at me. "Well," she replied, "I guess we'll just see what happens when that time comes! Thanks for coming by!"

I shook her hand and drove off to my next class.

Just a few weeks later, one of her co-workers left the company, and she had to pick up a lot of his portfolio. As it turns out, she later told me that she didn't even think once about the prophecy or the explanation. It wasn't until she left a staff meeting about a month later and prayed, "God, I don't know how I'm going to run this project! That guy's shoes are too big to fill!"

Within an instant, she remembered the message: "Big spiritual feet." Peace from the Holy Spirit overwhelmed her, and she moved forward with full confidence that her physical shortcomings would be matched with spiritual strength from the Lord.

One might wonder why I would call this a Word of Knowledge when it had to do with foretelling the future. But let's take another quick look at what transpired. The prophecy was that God had given the woman big spiritual feet. I simply conveyed a message the best way I knew how. The later explanation, however, was not a separate word of prophecy. I was no longer conveying a message, but rather expressing knowledge and understanding about the original message. I knew what Jesus meant as though I had meant it myself. The Holy Spirit took from Christ's knowledge and made it known to me. It was a Word of Knowledge.

Recognizing the Present Fulfillment of Prophecy

So far we've seen how the Word of Knowledge can pave the way for more effective prophecies. We've also seen how a Word of Knowledge can help us comprehend prophecy and make it more meaningful. Now I want to show you how the Word of Knowledge can help a person recognize the present fulfillment of prophecy.

In most cases, prophecies are proven and recognized as true only after the events foretold come to pass. Sometimes, though, it takes a Word of Knowledge to recognize when a prophecy is presently being fulfilled.

While still in Babylonian captivity, the prophet Daniel understood Jeremiah's prophecy. He recognized that the seventy years of captivity that were prophesied were about to end! Through a word of knowledge, Daniel understood when prophecy was about to be fulfilled rather than only noticing it after the fact. (See Daniel 9:2.)

Just before His final Passover feast, Jesus took the time to wash His disciples' feet. When He had finished washing the feet of His last disciple, Jesus joined them at the table and started to explain what had just taken place. Suddenly, though, His message took a dark turn.

"I am not referring to all of you; I know those I have chosen. But this is to fulfill the scripture: 'He who shares my bread has lifted up his heel against me.'

"I am telling you now before it happens, so that when it does happen you will believe that I am He..."

After he had said this, Jesus was troubled in spirit and testified, "I tell you the truth, one of you is going to betray me."

His disciples stared at one another, at a loss to know which of them he meant. One of them, [John], was reclining next to him. Simon Peter motioned to [him] and said, "Ask him which one he means."

Leaning back against Jesus, he asked him, "Lord, who is it?"

Jesus answered, "It is the one to whom I will give this piece of bread when I have dipped it in the dish." Then, dipping the piece of bread, he gave it to Judas Iscariot, son of Simon. As soon as Judas took the bread, satan entered into him.

"What you are about to do, do quickly," Jesus told him, but no one at the meal understood why Jesus said this to him (John 13:18-28).

Jesus started with prophecy—He quoted Psalm 41:9 as a means of foretelling the future. The purpose of the message was to strengthen, encourage, and comfort His disciples because He said that when it happens, they'll believe that He truly is the Messiah. As we learned earlier, a revelation from God that is spoken to strengthen, encourage, and comfort believers is a prophecy. And the fact that Jesus was foretelling the future was also a form of prophecy.

There was really no emotional connection to the message at this time—He was simply conveying a message that the Father had revealed to Him. But then it says that "after He said this, He was troubled in spirit and testified." That's when the

Word of Knowledge hit Him. He was no longer prophesying a message but suddenly had a download of what God the Father knew and felt for His Son. The events that His prophecy foretold were ready to transpire within mere moments.

Notice that when Jesus said, "One of you is going to betray Me," it wasn't any longer a matter of prophecy. Jesus wasn't just conveying a message that God had revealed. Rather, it says that He was deeply troubled in spirit and He "testified." In other words, He was explaining what He had suddenly witnessed. In an instant, Jesus knew without doubt that it was time for the Scriptures to be fulfilled.

As an eyewitness, John remembered vividly the shift in Jesus' emotions and demeanor. He noticed something changed after Jesus prophesied a message for the group's comfort. He saw the moment when Jesus was suddenly troubled in spirit. The Word of Knowledge itself would have been impressive enough on its own. But the prophecy preceding it gave the moment that much more weight. Not everyone understood exactly what was taking place, but the young apostle named John was certainly impacted by it.

The "More Certain" Word of Prophecy

As we've seen, the Gift of Prophecy is expressed in various ways. It's always for the benefit of a group or individual, and it's always a message from God. Sometimes it has to do with what God says about the past, sometimes what He says about the present, and sometimes it's a promise or prediction about the future.

It's easy to get wrapped up in the present-day expressions of this gift and overlook the ancient ones that still have meaning to us. I'm talking, of course, about the Bible. Peter called the Scriptures *"the word of the prophets made more certain"* (2 Peter 1:19). The words of Scripture have been proven true throughout time and are still meaningful to us in today's world and culture. So if we take the perspective that the Bible is a form of prophecy, then we see how our examples of the Word of Knowledge apply.

For instance, have you ever been reading the Bible and had something click for you? When it happens, it feels like something suddenly makes sense that had never really come together for you before. One little verse reveals the big picture, and it's like fireworks go off in your heart. Has that ever happened?

This is what we call a "revelation," and it's part of the Word of Knowledge. In the previous chapter, I shared a story about suddenly knowing information as though I had been there to witness it. That too was a revelation. It didn't become a Word of Knowledge, though, until I spoke it out.

Paul said that the purpose of spiritual gifts is *"for the common good."* (See 1 Corinthians 12:7.) So as long as I keep something bottled up inside, it's only a gift to me. But if we want it to be a spiritual gift to the Church, then it needs to be articulated.

The same thing goes for a revelation born out of Scripture. When it's spoken in order to strengthen others, the message goes from being mere internal revelation and becomes a Word of Knowledge.

Perhaps the most practical example I can offer you is this book itself. As you may recall, I was reading Jesus' words about the Holy Spirit when the gifts of the Spirit suddenly made sense to me. In one instant, the Holy Spirit unfolded a Scripturally-based definition for every spiritual gift in the Bible. Something Jesus has known and understood from the beginning of time was somehow made known to me as I read the Scripture. That's a revelation.

I could have sat on that information, and it would have been very satisfying for me personally. My frustrations in seeking for a sensible, biblically sound definition for the Word of Knowledge would have been alleviated! But alas, God's revelations rarely work like that. Instead, I found myself like Jeremiah:

> *But if I say, "I will not mention him or speak any more in his name," his word is in my heart like a fire, a fire shut up in my bones. I am weary of holding it in; indeed, I cannot* (Jeremiah 20:9).

It's a joy to share revelation (and many times, a relief)! The Church can be edified when we articulate what the Holy Spirit has revealed.

Why is the Church edified? There are practical reasons: we understand God's Word better, we understand God better, and we're encouraged in our faith. But there's also a supernatural reason: if the Holy Spirit reveals something to you that came from Jesus, you don't just understand information—you have experienced Jesus! And when you convey that revelation to the Church, we all get a glimpse of Jesus! I didn't write this book so you can just learn information; I did it because I want you to encounter an aspect of our Lord that has previously seldom been discussed.

Jesus is the Head of the Church; and the better we all know and understand Him, the easier it is for those of us in His Body to function in unity! To receive a spiritual revelation from the Scripture is to receive a spiritual revelation of Christ Himself! You cannot separate the Scripture from the Word of God; and Jesus is the Word of God!

Jesus is the Word of God

If you've read the Gospel of John, you know that Jesus is the Word of God. John starts his book by saying, *"In the beginning was the Word, and the Word was with God, and the Word was God..."* (John 1:1). In other words, Jesus was present at creation. In fact, not only was He present, but He was the means by which everything was created!

> *For by him all things were created: things in heaven and on earth, visible and invisible, whether thrones or powers or rulers or authorities; all things were created by him and for him* (Colossians 1:16).

And when we read Genesis, we find that the entire universe was spoken into existence by God. God's Word created everything, and Jesus is the Word of God.

Not only this, but we see yet another example in the book of Genesis. After Adam and Eve committed their first carnal sin, they realized they were naked and hid in the bushes.

And they heard the voice of Jehovah God walking in the garden in the cool of the day... (Genesis 3:8 ASV).

Other versions say "sound" instead of "voice," but this is a very valid translation from the original Hebrew text. The voice of God was walking! That means God's voice had form! Jesus—the Word of God—is found all throughout the Scripture! Then we find that Peter wrote this:

Above all, you must understand that no prophecy of Scripture came about by the prophet's own interpretation. For prophecy never had its origin in the will of man, but men spoke from God as they were carried along by the Holy Spirit (2 Peter 1:20-21).

Scripture is prophecy, which is another gift of the Spirit. "Men spoke from God" through the Holy Spirit! In other words, the Holy Spirit took from the Father and made it known to human beings. And what was the message? The Word of God! Who is the Word of God in the flesh? Jesus! All of Scripture is a prophecy, and so all of Scripture reveals Jesus!

...the testimony of Jesus is the spirit of prophecy (Revelation 19:10b).

All prophecy—and therefore all Scripture—reveals Jesus Christ. He is the Word of God. This is how all the gifts of the Spirit work—the Holy Spirit reveals some part of Jesus to someone in the Church, and that person becomes a vessel through whom the rest of the Church then encounters Him. The gifts of the Spirit are "for the common good."

The Word of Knowledge, Prophecy, and Scripture Working Together

Perhaps the most well-known prophetic message throughout Scripture is the hundreds of Old Testament prophecies pointing to one Person: Jesus Christ. The Old Testament is chock-full of prophecies about the Messiah—how He would come, how He would live, how He would die, and how He would win ultimate victory in the end!

So when the angel appeared to the virgin Mary to say that she would bear this child, it wasn't just a random occurrence. Rather, there were thousands of years of prophecies to back up everything that would take place! And these weren't just prophecies that were spoken out and forgotten; they were prophetic declarations that were written in songs, letters, history books, poetry, and more—all of which became sacred Scripture over time.

Soon after Mary's miraculous conception of Jesus, she went to visit her cousin Elizabeth. Here we see two clear examples of a Word of Knowledge expressing an understanding of Scripture and the present fulfillment of prophecy.

When Elizabeth heard Mary's greeting, the baby leaped in her womb, and Elizabeth was filled with the Holy Spirit. In a loud voice she exclaimed: "Blessed are you among women, and blessed is the child you will bear! But why am I so favored, that the mother of my Lord should come to me? As soon as the sound of your greeting reached my ears, the baby in my womb leaped for joy. Blessed is she who has believed

that what the Lord has said to her will be accomplished!"
(Luke 1:40-45).

First, little baby John the Baptist—who was himself a fulfillment of prophecy—recognized the presence of the Messiah for whom he would become a forerunner, even while they were both still inside their mothers' wombs! Before he even had the words and logic to articulate what was happening, John expressed the excitement in his heart about what he knew to be true as a result of spiritual revelation. The Word of Knowledge requires clear communication of the point but doesn't necessarily have to be spoken in words. John the Baptist communicated to his mother that something was special about this cousin and her baby!

Then comes the even clearer example of a Word of Knowledge. Elizabeth is filled with the Holy Spirit and proclaims about Mary what she now knows to be true! When everyone else probably thought Mary was lying about her "virgin conception," this cousin of hers had a Word of Knowledge that brought vindication from the Lord! Not only that, but it showed a realization that the prophecies of Scripture were coming to clear fulfillment!

Prophecy is the Word of God, the Bible is the Word of God, and Jesus is the Word of God. Therefore, a Word of Knowledge regarding prophecy or Scripture is actually a direct look into the thoughts and intentions of God in Jesus. To have a Word of Knowledge about the Word of God is not just to understand Scripture, but to commune with the divine Author of that Scripture. It is to experience Jesus Christ! Through revelation from the Holy Spirit, Jesus shares Himself with us!

The Word of Knowledge is a spiritual gift that powerfully unveils the person of Christ.

Summary Questions

1. What are the basic differences between the gift of Prophecy and the gift of a Word of Knowledge?

   _____

   _____

2. What are some ways that the Word of Knowledge interacts with the gift of Prophecy?

   _____

   _____

3. What did Peter call "the word of the prophets made more certain"?

   _____

   _____

4. Who is the Word of God?

   _____

   _____

Chapter 3

the word of knowledge and visions and dreams ↗

Everything the Holy Spirit does brings glory to Jesus Christ. Jesus is the source and reality behind all spiritual and natural created things. (See Colossians 1:16-20.) So no matter what gift of the Spirit is in operation, Jesus is at the center of it.

When it comes to visions and dreams, all true revelation comes from Jesus because He is the Word of God.

> *This is what the Lord Almighty says: "Do not listen to what the prophets are prophesying to you; they fill you with false hopes. They speak visions from their own minds, not from the mouth of the Lord* (Jeremiah 23:16).

Did you catch that? True visions come from the mouth of the Lord! Remember, Jesus is the Word of God; so a true vision comes as a result of Jesus!

I like to think about it this way: First John 1:5 says that God is light and in Him is no darkness at all. Furthermore, in John 8:12, Jesus said, *"I am the light of the world. Whoever follows Me will never walk in darkness, but will have the light of life."* Keep that in mind.

In the natural realm, the only reason we can see things is because light bounces off objects, enters our eyes, and is processed by our brains. The less light there is, the more difficult it is for us to discern exactly where we are or what we're looking at.

Jesus answered, "Are there not twelve hours of daylight? A man who walks by day will not stumble, for he sees by this world's light. It is when he walks by night that he stumbles, for he has no light" (John 11:9-10).

The spiritual light of Jesus works the same way. The light of who He is reveals things in the spiritual realm that are perceived and processed in our spirit. Visions are just one natural result of being in the Light, which is the Word of God—Jesus. It only stands to reason, then, that a Word of Knowledge will often work in conjunction with visions and dreams.

There's an Italian restaurant in my area that has two big lion sculptures outside the front door. At first glance, they look like marble, but I honestly never expected them to be. Why spend the money to make them out of marble when there are modern plastics that can give the exact same effect? So out of curiosity one day, I walked over to one and felt it. Sure enough, the statue was solid marble.

The Greeks of Bible times would say that I didn't "know" the lion was made of marble until I experienced it. Even though it looked like marble, I couldn't truly testify that it was made of marble until I actually knew through personal contact.

Likewise, when it comes to visions and dreams of spiritual things, interpretations are one thing, but knowing is another! One can have an ability to interpret dreams and visions, but a Word of Knowledge is something deeper. Why? Because a Word of Knowledge is the ability to share some of Christ's knowledge! I'm talking about the same Christ who actually is the light of revelation in that moment! Whereas an interpretation is a revelation from the Holy Spirit that expresses the meaning, a Word of Knowledge is a revelation of the Holy Spirit by which one can have full understanding. The person receiving the Word of Knowledge understands the message of the vision as though he had painted the picture himself.

Visions come from the mouth of God. They are pictorial expressions unveiled by Jesus. Who knows better what is meant in a vision or dream than the one who originally authored it, expressed it, and revealed it?

There are many ways in which a Word of Knowledge can work in conjunction with visions and dreams. Sometimes the Word of Knowledge comes in the form of a vision or dream. Other times, the vision or dream gives us insight into a Word of Knowledge. And still other times, the Word of Knowledge helps us understand a vision or dream. All of these are ways that Jesus makes part of Himself known among us.

The Word of Knowledge Accompanying a Vision or Dream

There are times when Jesus shares His knowledge through a vision or dream and other times when He shares His knowledge with an accompanying vision or dream.

71

In Acts 9, we meet a man named Saul who was bent on persecuting and killing a particular cult of Jews who were putting their faith in some "Messiah-figure" named Jesus. On his way to a city called Damascus, where he planned to capture some of these cult followers, Saul's entourage was halted abruptly! A light from Heaven whipped around Saul, and he fell to the ground.

He…heard a voice say to him, "Saul, Saul, why do you persecute me?"

"Who are you, Lord?" Saul asked.

"I am Jesus, whom you are persecuting," he replied. "Now get up and go into the city, and you will be told what you must do."

The men traveling with Saul stood there speechless; they heard the sound but did not see anyone. Saul got up from the ground, but when he opened his eyes he could see nothing. So they led him by the hand into Damascus. For three days he was blind, and did not eat or drink anything.

In Damascus there was a disciple named Ananias. The Lord called to him in a vision, "Ananias!"

"Yes, Lord," he answered.

The Lord told him, "Go to the house of Judas on Straight Street and ask for a man from Tarsus named Saul, for he is praying. In a vision he has seen a man named Ananias come and place his hands on him to restore his sight."

"Lord," Ananias answered, "I have heard many reports about this man and all the harm he has done to your saints

in Jerusalem. And he has come here with authority from the chief priests to arrest all who call on your name."

But the Lord said to Ananias, "Go! This man is my chosen instrument to carry my name before the Gentiles and their kings and before the people of Israel. I will show him how much he must suffer for my name."

Then Ananias went to the house and entered it. Placing his hands on Saul, he said, "Brother Saul, the Lord—Jesus, who appeared to you on the road as you were coming here—has sent me so that you may see again and be filled with the Holy Spirit." Immediately, something like scales fell from Saul's eyes, and he could see again. He got up and was baptized, and after taking some food, he regained his strength.

Saul spent several days with the disciples in Damascus. At once he began to preach in the synagogues that Jesus is the Son of God. All those who heard him were astonished and asked, "Isn't he the man who raised havoc in Jerusalem among those who call on this name? And hasn't he come here to take them as prisoners to the chief priests?" Yet Saul grew more and more powerful and baffled the Jews living in Damascus by proving that Jesus is the Christ (Acts 9:4-22).

In a vision, a disciple named Ananias was given very clear information. First he was told an exact location; then he was given the name of the man for whom he was looking. Furthermore, he was told clearly what this man had already seen in a vision. Of course Jesus knew what Saul had seen because He was the one who revealed it to him!

Something I find interesting is that Jesus never told Ananias that He had appeared to Saul on the road to Damascus, but Ananias shared this information as though he was fully aware! Furthermore, Jesus didn't say that Saul had to be filled with the Holy Spirit, but Ananias knew that this must take place. Here we see a vision and a Word of Knowledge working in conjunction. Jesus gave clear information to Ananias, but it wasn't just a string of words. Along with it came a full understanding of what had taken place and what must come next.

I was once serving on staff at a retreat hosted by three different churches. During the first couple days of sessions and ministry times, one of the young men under my direct care had received dramatic deliverance from an evil spirit and healing in his heart from many hurts in his past.

When Sunday came, while we were eating breakfast at the camp's cafeteria, the young man flagged me over to his table. He was on the phone with his girlfriend back home, trying to explain all the exciting things God had done in his heart that weekend. But during their conversation, the girl's brother started pounding on her locked bedroom door and threatening her in a voice she'd never heard before. The young man told me this story with fear in his eyes and asked what to do.

Instantly, through a Word of Knowledge, I knew exactly what needed to take place. I said with absolute certainty, "Give me two minutes."

"What if you're wrong?" he asked.

"If at any point while I'm gone he comes in her door, I want you to hang up and call the police for her, but that's not going to happen. And if he hasn't left when two minutes are up, then she can call the police herself. Two minutes."

I ran out of the busy cafeteria, dashed around the corner, and dove to the ground between two empty bunk houses. I prayed passionately for God to bring deliverance and peace in this girl's household.

Within a matter of seconds, the Holy Spirit opened my spiritual eyes to a vision of what was taking place. Through pictures in my mind, I saw into the hallway of that girl's house. I could see a painting on the wall, the color of the carpet, and a huge, billowing, swirling black cloud pounding violently on a door to the right. I spoke to that spirit as though it was right in front of me and said, "In the name of Jesus, leave her alone."

The churning of the cloud continued, so I said again, "Leave in the name of Jesus! Holy Spirit, I ask You to bring peace into this house."

In an instant, the black cloud seemed to be sucked into a room at the end of the hallway, and the door slammed shut.

I glanced down at my watch and saw I had about fifteen seconds to run back into the cafeteria. I burst through the doors at exactly two minutes, only to see the young man staring at me with his jaw hanging open.

"What happened?" I asked.

"Just a few seconds ago, she said her brother screamed, ran to his bedroom at the end of the hall, and slammed the door shut. She said that she feels peace in her room like never before. What did you do?"

"It's not a matter of what I did," I replied, "it's all about what God did. Jesus was there to see the whole thing happening, and it was His authority and His Spirit that brought peace." I explained the picture I saw hanging and the color of the carpet, which he confirmed to be true. He then handed me his phone, and I had the privilege of sharing the Gospel with the young woman.

Through a vision, the Holy Spirit gave me knowledge of what was happening in that girl's house as though I was actually there. And as Jesus shared something He knew with me, I also knew exactly what to do and say in His name.

Eyewitnesses through Spiritual Revelation

This concept of seeing an actual remote location through spiritual revelation seems strange to some. New age and occult religions talk about "remote viewing," and so we Christians are often leery of such concepts.

We have to realize that satan isn't creative. He doesn't invent new abilities for human beings—he merely perverts and counterfeits what God has already designed. There was a time when the Christian population at large was leery of the Word of Knowledge itself because it looked a lot like the psychics who were receiving information from evil spirits.

Counterfeits are just imitations of the real deal. No one would go to the trouble of making a counterfeit seventeen dollar bill because it would never pass as the real thing. But make a counterfeit twenty, and you might get away with something shady.

The same goes in the spiritual realm. Satan didn't invent the gifts of the Holy Spirit; he only perverts, twists, and counterfeits them to distract people from the true God. So when it comes to seeing remote locations through a vision or dream, this is something God has been doing for millennia, of which the devil merely tries to make a cheap imitation.

One of my favorite instances of this in the Bible comes from the prophet Elisha. The king of Aram had a commander in his army, Naaman, who had a skin condition called leprosy. After receiving a tip from an Israeli servant girl, Naaman set out to find the prophet of God who could heal him of his leprosy.

Naaman brought with him the modern-day equivalent of about $200,000 in silver and about $2.5 million in gold. He also brought 10 sets of clothing, which I'm sure were some pretty spiffy duds, considering the wealth this man had at his disposal.

To make a long story short, Naaman and his chariots rode to the door of Elisha's house, and Elisha sent a messenger out to tell Naaman to wash himself seven times in the Jordan River.

Naaman was insulted that Elisha hadn't come out in person, and he knew that the Jordan river was nasty compared to the rivers he had back in his homeland. But with some coaxing from his entourage, Naaman finally followed the instructions, and after seven dips, stepped out of the Jordan River completely healed!

Then Naaman and his entire party went back to find the man of God. They stood before him, and Naaman said, "Now I know that there is no God in all the world except in Israel. So please accept a gift from your servant."

But Elisha replied, "As surely as the Lord lives, whom I serve, I will not accept any gifts." And though Naaman urged him to take the gift, Elisha refused (2 Kings 5:15-16 NLT).

With Elisha's blessing, Naaman headed back home with all his gifts of silver, gold, and fine clothing.

But Elisha had a servant named Gehazi who saw all these events transpire. Gehazi was shocked that Elisha would let a man who was willing to give so much wealth walk away without leaving so much as a penny. He thought Elisha had gone too easy on him and snuck off to get a piece of the pie.

When Naaman saw Gehazi running after him, he climbed down from his chariot and went to meet him. "Is everything all right?" Naaman asked.

"Yes," Gehazi said, "but my master has sent me to tell you that two young prophets from the hill country of Ephraim have just arrived. He would like 75 pounds of silver [today worth over $20,000] and two sets of clothing to give to them."

"By all means, take twice as much silver," Naaman insisted. He gave him two sets of clothing, tied up the money in two bags, and sent two of his servants to carry the gifts for Gehazi. But when they arrived at the citadel, Gehazi took

the gifts from the servants and sent the men back. Then he went and hid the gifts inside the house.

When he went in to his master, Elisha asked him, "Where have you been, Gehazi?"

"I haven't been anywhere," he replied.

But Elisha asked him, "Don't you realize that I was there in spirit when Naaman stepped down from his chariot to meet you? Is this the time to receive money and clothing, olive groves and vineyards, sheep and cattle, and male and female servants? Because you have done this, you and your descendants will suffer from Naaman's leprosy forever." When Gehazi left the room, he was covered with leprosy; his skin was white as snow (2 Kings 5:21b-27 NLT).

While still in his house, Elisha saw the entire event take place in his spirit. God simply revealed it to him. Elisha had a Word of Knowledge by which God enabled him to be an eye-witness of something that couldn't have been seen apart from spiritual revelation. In this case, the vision was the means by which Elisha received a Word of Knowledge.

Jesus did this too. In John 1:47-50, Jesus called Nathaniel to be His disciple. He spoke clearly about the condition of Nathaniel's heart and shared how He had seen Nathaniel under a fig tree before Philip called him to come see Jesus. This astonished Nathaniel and shook him to the core.

There are a couple possible reasons for this. First, it could simply be that Nathaniel was somewhere that he couldn't be seen and was amazed that Jesus knew what had happened under the fig tree—whatever that may have been. The second possibility is that Jesus was using a common idiom from that time period. To say, "I saw you under the fig tree," was the ancient Israel equivalent of saying, "I knew you since you were 'this big.'" In this way, Jesus would have been saying, "I know your entire life, Nathaniel." Whichever the case, it impacted Nathaniel enough to declare, "Teacher, You're the Son of God—the King of Israel!"

Jesus had a Word of Knowledge about Nathaniel's character that was born out of a vision in which He saw Nathaniel when nobody else was looking.

Remember Saul from our story earlier? In case you didn't know, he soon changed his name to Paul and became the apostle who wrote roughly half of the New Testament. In a couple of his letters, Paul expressed that even though he couldn't be physically present, he was there in spirit to see everything. Then he would comment or pass judgment as though he had actually been a physical eyewitness.

Even though I am not physically present, I am with you in spirit. And I have already passed judgment on the one who did this, just as if I were present. When you are assembled in the name of our Lord Jesus and I am with you in spirit, and the power of our Lord Jesus is present, hand this man over to Satan, so that the sinful nature may be destroyed and his spirit saved on the day of the Lord (1 Corinthians 5:3-5).

For though I am absent from you in body, I am present with you in spirit and delight to see how orderly you are and how firm your faith in Christ is (Colossians 2:5).

80

Paul also received a Word of Knowledge based on a vision in which he saw someone in a distant land.

During the night Paul had a vision of a man of Macedonia standing and begging him, "Come over to Macedonia and help us." After Paul had seen the vision, we got ready at once to leave for Macedonia, concluding that God had called us to preach the gospel to them (Acts 16:9-10).

Paul received a Word of Knowledge that gave him clear understanding of who was ready to receive the Gospel next. It came in the form of a vision, and it played a key role in directing the next step in his missionary journey.

The Word of Knowledge can often come in conjunction with a vision or dream. Other times, as we'll see in a moment, it can be simply prompted by a vision or dream.

Visions that Prompt a Word of Knowledge

Before my wife Robin and I were married, I went to her parents' house to have dinner and spend the evening together. When I arrived, though, her parents were out getting food. A young lady from one of Robin's college classes was there instead. Something didn't feel right, so I started asking the Lord what was wrong so I could minister to her.

Robin introduced me to the young lady, and we started making small talk. All the while, I was trying to remain sensitive to the Holy Spirit. Then, not with my physical eyes but in my spirit, I saw an angel standing behind the young lady, and he opened up a scroll that was facing me.

I couldn't read anything on the scroll, so I was really wondering just what God was trying to say. Why was Jesus revealing this to me? It was His light, after all, which made this vision possible. I started asking the Lord what this was about.

Then it suddenly struck me. I realized that the scroll was facing me because God wanted to reveal things to me. I concluded that whatever came to my mind in that moment would be a Word of Knowledge, so I started talking.

Intricate details of a recent troubling breakup with a young man came to mind. I expressed what she had gone through and what she had thought about God in the midst of all this. I also expressed what God thought about her and everything that had taken place. It was perhaps the most long-winded and accurate Word of Knowledge I've ever received, and I probably wouldn't have had the faith to keep talking if it hadn't been for the vision of the angel with the scroll. When the vision stopped, I stopped and transitioned naturally into praying for her and explaining the Gospel.

Through that Word of Knowledge, this young lady received Jesus, started attending church, and had her heart healed from the devastation of that nasty breakup. But, as I said, I probably wouldn't have had the faith to share so many details without the vision that accompanied the revelation. Visions and dreams can therefore occasionally be fuel for the Word of Knowledge.

I think also of the Jewish patriarch Jacob:

When he reached a certain place, he stopped for the night because the sun had set. Taking one of the stones there, he put it under his head and lay down to sleep. He had a dream in which he saw a stairway resting on the earth, with its top reaching to heaven, and the angels of God were ascending and descending on it. There above it stood the Lord, and he said: "I am the Lord, the God of your father Abraham and the God of Isaac. I will give you and your descendants the land on which you are lying. Your descendants will be like the dust of the earth, and you will spread out to the west and to the east, to the north and to the south. All peoples on earth will be blessed through you and your offspring. I am with you and will watch over you wherever you go, and I will bring you back to this land. I will not leave you until I have done what I have promised you."

When Jacob awoke from his sleep, he thought, "Surely the Lord is in this place, and I was not aware of it." He was afraid and said, "How awesome is this place! This is none other than the house of God; this is the gate of heaven" (Genesis 28:11-17).

Jacob had a dream that said nothing about the place where he was, yet he woke up with the knowledge that he was on very holy ground! Jacob took the stone he had used as a pillow and stood it on end like a pillar to mark the site. Then he named the place "Bethel," which means "House of God." Jacob's dream prompted a Word of Knowledge, which in turn prompted a prophetic act that spoke destiny into an entire region for years to come.

Bringing Understanding of Dreams and Visions

There are also cases in which a Word of Knowledge is necessary to accurately understand a dream or vision. As I said in the beginning of this chapter, interpretation is merely a spiritual gift in which the Holy Spirit reveals the meaning Jesus intended in the vision or dream. But the Word of Knowledge actually brings a person into fuller understanding.

Someone once came to me, very troubled about a dream involving a snake and her parents. As she explained what she had seen, the woman then started to go into detail about how she was afraid that it meant the enemy was about to do something horrible in her family.

This didn't quite settle right in my heart, so I asked the Holy Spirit to give me insight. I then suddenly saw a vision of the dream she'd had.

"Was it a red snake?" I asked.

"Yes! How did you know?"

"And when you looked at this snake, you didn't have any fear, did you?"

"No! I actually felt really calm. What does this mean?"

"Well," I continued, "Snakes don't always represent the devil. They also can represent Christ. Moses hoisted a bronze snake up a pole for the Israelites to look at and be healed, and Jesus said this was a prophetic symbol of Himself. (See

Numbers 21:4-9 and John 3:14-15.) This snake was red because it represents the blood of Christ. The dream actually means that Jesus is about to bring healing in your family."

Sure enough, within a couple months, this woman's family was miraculously restored by a work of the Holy Spirit. Her parents tore up some divorce papers that were waiting to be signed, and God started changing their family dynamic for the better.

In this case, knowing the meanings behind symbols had to do with a gift of interpretation, but it took a Word of Knowledge to experience what she had seen in her dream and bring deeper understanding.

The prophet Daniel had an even more amazing experience. The king of Babylon, Nebuchadnezzar, had a dream that deeply troubled him.

King Nebuchadnezzar called for all the assumedly "spiritual" people in his kingdom—sorcerers, magicians, enchanters, and astrologers—to come divine what his dream was. He didn't just want an interpretation; he wanted them to actually tell him the dream! Nebuchadnezzar suspected that his magicians weren't really hearing from "the gods," which would mean that they had been telling him misleading information and pushing their own agendas. Surely, if they could divine the dream, they would have the true interpretation to go with it.

Of course, none of them could do such a thing! If it's the light of Christ that reveals spiritual images, and if it's true that in Him there is no darkness at all, then how could the kingdom of darkness have any insight into what was seen?

How could sorcerers and enchanters possibly receive that information from their usual demons? Obviously, they couldn't tell what the dream was, and the men expressed that they couldn't believe the king would ask something so impossible of them.

The king was so enraged that he called for every wise man in Babylon to be killed! But Daniel, the young Hebrew eunuch who already had a knack for interpreting dreams through the Holy Spirit, came to the king and asked for more time.

With the king's death-sentence momentarily stayed, Daniel hurried back to his house and explained everything to his three friends. They sought the true God—the God of light and revelation who originally authored the dream—and pleaded for His help.

During the night the mystery was revealed to Daniel in a vision. Then Daniel praised the God of heaven and said: "Praise be to the name of God for ever and ever; wisdom and power are his.

He changes times and seasons; he sets up kings and deposes them. He gives wisdom to the wise and knowledge to the discerning.

He reveals deep and hidden things; he knows what lies in darkness, and light dwells with him.

I thank and praise you, O God of my fathers: You have given me wisdom and power, you have made known to me what we asked of you, you have made known to us the dream of the king" (Daniel 2:19-23).

Daniel received a Word of Knowledge about the King's Dream through a vision. Had it not been for the revelation of the Holy Spirit, Daniel and his friends would have been put to death; but God brought a Word of Knowledge to Daniel in a vision, which allowed him to experience the dream as though he had dreamt it himself! In verse 29, Daniel gives us an exciting name for God: the Revealer of Mysteries.

This Revealer of Mysteries who we serve is the One who sheds light on things otherwise unseen. The revelation we receive from Him is such that no demon can share in the knowledge! Through the Holy Spirit, we can discern things with greater accuracy than the cheap imitations whom the world calls "psychics." Not only that, but our revelation is not just of information or trivia; it presents Jesus, the Word of God, as well! The Word of Knowledge is a means by which we can personally introduce Jesus to a spiritually hungry people.

One of my wife's co-workers started talking about her house being haunted. She was living with her boyfriend and his two children, and the kids were seeing things, talking to "ghosts," and screaming and crying in the middle of the night. They would hear footsteps, the dead bolt on their door would click back and forth, and the entire family kept hearing voices.

My wife, Robin, invited the woman to tell me everything that was happening, and I calmly said, "That's nothing crazy. If you ever want it to go away, just let us know. We're Christians, so we know how to take care of stuff like that."

The woman laughed it off as though I was kidding. "You bet!" she chuckled.

Sure enough, about two weeks later, my phone rang on a Sunday afternoon.

"Remember what you said about making all this stuff stop? This morning my boyfriend woke up in a cold sweat with a painful bite mark on his arm, and the kids don't want to live here anymore. I took them to their grandparents' house for the night. How soon can you come?"

After asking if it was alright to invite others, I grabbed my wife and four solid Christian friends and headed over to the house.

On the way, I started praying that God would reveal exactly what was happening. Fifteen minutes away, I had a vision of an old man and a little girl. I asked the Lord to show me more, and the two figures each reached up and grabbed a stick that hung down from their chins. Off came a mask. When the masks were removed, I saw two demons laughing and pointing as though making fun of someone.

"What does this mean?" I asked.

Then the Lord started unfolding a bit of the interpretation.

We pulled up to the house and went inside. I started by explaining that this wasn't going to go like some Hollywood movie with stuff flying all over the place and heads spinning. I said that the authority of Christ is more powerful than any evil spirit, so even if something did start happening, we can just tell it to stop, and it will.

Then I said, "I'm not going to tell these spirits to leave today. Based on the way you're living, if I do that, they'll just come back with more demons, and you'll be in worse shape than you are now. (See Matthew 12:43-45 and Luke 11:24-26.)

"If you were to place a pile of sugar in front of your door," I explained, "it will attract ants. You can yell at the ants all you want, but they won't leave because you've created an environment that invites them into your house. Likewise, the two of you are living in darkness, and that's like sugar in front of the door for evil spirits. The reason these spirits have access to your house is because you've invited them in with your lifestyles."

I went on to explain the Gospel to them, and a few of us shared our testimonies of what Christ had done in our lives.

"But how do we know that what you're saying is true?" begged the woman. "What if this has nothing to do with the ghosts in our house? How do we know you can actually fix this?"

Then I explained the vision I had about the old man and the little girl.

The couple sitting on the couch looked at me in shock, and the man interrupted, "That's what my boys keep seeing!" He started to tell specific stories about recent encounters with two "ghosts" that looked like an old man and a little girl.

As it turns out, the vision I had in the car was a Word of Knowledge by which I saw what they had been seeing. But because I was seeing with the light of Christ, I knew an extra detail that they didn't know about.

"Well, they're not ghosts," I replied. I explained the masks and the laughing demons behind them. "They're what I would call 'mocking spirits,' and they're mocking you two."

"How?" asked the intrigued couple in unison.

I actually wasn't prepared for that question, but then I had another Word of Knowledge. Pointing to the man, I said, "The old man is mocking you..." and pointing to the woman, I added, "and the little girl is mocking you."

I looked back at the man and said, "Three years ago, you were a strong Christian, but you gave all that up to take up the lifestyle of your 'old man.'" (The "old man" was a term Paul used in reference to the former sinful way of life.) (See Romans 6:6, Ephesians 4:22, and Colossians 3:9 in the King James Version.)

The man was shocked and affirmed that everything that was said had been true.

Turning back to the woman, I said, "And the spirit masquerading as a little girl is mocking you. You were raised in a Christian home, but something traumatic happened when you were a little girl that stunted your spiritual growth. As a result, you always see yourself as a scared little girl."

The woman sobbed on my wife's shoulder and nodded her head. The Lord revealed further details about what had happened, and the woman experienced emotional healing from the Lord as we prayed.

I explained once again that I wasn't going to tell the spirits to leave for the reasons noted earlier. But I did feel that we had permission from the Lord to tell them to be silent in the house for the sake of the boys returning home and not being afraid.

I also urged the couple not to make a hasty decision about the Gospel.

"This is a life-altering decision," I said, "and I don't want you to just jump in on some emotional high. If you want to follow Christ, then you're going to have to stop sleeping together, change your entertainment choices, and dedicate yourselves to a relationship with Jesus. This will affect your entire lives as you know them. So tonight and tomorrow, I want you to talk about it and make a solid decision. If you want to follow Christ, then come to our small group meeting tomorrow night so we can talk about it."

The next night, I got a call. The boys, completely unaware of what had transpired the night before, returned home to a peaceful house. The woman told me that the three-year-old had been walking around the house for hours asking, "Where's the little girl? I can't find the little girl?" The couple knew that everything that was happening was true; and so they came, committed their lives to Christ, and started attending our small group and a local church every week.

The story doesn't stop there, but I'll finish it in another chapter. For now, simply know that God can give you a Word of Knowledge that will radically impact a family with the Truth of Christ. That whole family encountered Jesus, and He changed them forever!

The Word of Knowledge doesn't have to involve visions and dreams, but this is a very common way in which this spiritual gift can work. A Word of Knowledge comes from the Word of God, and visions come from the mouth of God, so it should come as no surprise that they often work in conjunction.

Summary Questions

1. According to Jeremiah 23:16, where do true visions come from?

    _____

    _____

2. Describe the correlation between natural sight and spiritual sight. Who is the "Light" for the believer?

    _____

    _____

3. What is the difference between true visions, dreams, and Words of Knowledge versus varying occult practices like psychic readings and astral projection (a.k.a. "remote viewing")?

    _____

    _____

4. Who is the "Revealer of Mysteries"?

    _____

    _____

Chapter 4

the word of knowledge and physical healing ↗

When my wife, Robin, and I were still in high school, our church youth group used to go out every Wednesday night after church to eat at a local restaurant. It wasn't long before we met Andrea—a waitress who was only slightly older than us and already had an infant at home. She, her baby, and her boyfriend were all living at her mother's house and struggling to make ends meet.

Week after week, we requested her. We would share the Gospel with her and always made it a point to over-tip (showing Christ's love in a more practical way). We bought a Bible for her and a box of diapers for the baby. Andrea was an ongoing ministry for several months before she left that restaurant.

One night, as I was driving from church to the restaurant, I was praying for Andrea. A picture popped into my mind in which I saw her with a brace on her right hand. *Wouldn't it be awesome*, I thought, *if we got there and she had a brace on her right hand? I would have unshakable faith that God wanted to heal her!*

Robin and I pulled up to the restaurant at the same time and went inside together. As you can imagine, the first thing I did was scan the restaurant for Andrea, specifically looking for her hand. But when I spotted her, there was no brace. With the wind sucked from my sails, we sat down in Andrea's section just in time for her to approach our table.

"How's it going, Andrea?" I asked.

"Fine," she answered, "Except that I smashed my hand! I'm sure it's broken."

I didn't know whether to be excited or feel stupid for not just asking, "How's your hand?" But before I could react, Andrea put her hand out in front of us to show us the damage. The whole hand was black and blue—badly swollen and moderately disfigured. Unfortunately for Andrea, she usually carried her tray on her right hand, so this was severely impairing her ability to work.

"This may sound really strange to you," I started, "but I had a vision about this on the way here, and I think it means God wants to heal your hand. Is it alright if we pray for you?"

A little stunned, she replied with a nervous laugh, "Sure, why not."

Robin, who I knew had a gift of healing, gently placed her hands on Andrea's wrist and prayed. And can you guess what happened?

Nothing!

I was actually more shocked that she didn't get healed than I would have been if she had come out totally fine! If we had kept on praying, something would have probably eventually happened (as is now my experience), but at the time, that was all I knew to do. I was certain that I had received a Word of Knowledge, but for some reason there didn't seem to be any power to back up what had transpired.

"Oh well," Andrea shrugged, and she took our drink orders. When the rest of our friends arrived, I shared with them what had happened and how confused I was that she wasn't healed. Several people shared thoughts, but we never really reached a conclusion.

That is, until we said grace. While praying for our food, we asked the Lord to reveal what might be hindering the healing that He obviously wanted to perform. That's when one of my friends and I both had a Word of Knowledge at the same time. We both sensed that God was first interested with the reason she broke her hand and wanted to perform more than just a physical healing.

When she came back, we lovingly confronted her—which was easy considering the relationship we had all built with her in the previous weeks. Andrea openly confessed that she hurt her hand while fighting with her boyfriend.

"I'll tell you what," I said in faith, "Go home, tell your boyfriend that you shouldn't be living together, and that he either needs to marry you or move out in the next week. It will be hard, but you'll know that you did the right thing because God will instantly heal your hand."

The next week we stepped into the restaurant just in time to see Andrea walking by with a full tray balanced high on her right hand.

"Looks like you got things worked out at home!" I said excitedly.

Andrea glanced at her hand and smiled, "Yeah."

Physical Healing and Spiritual Roots

In the previous story, God used a Word of Knowledge to promise a physical healing, and then He used the healing to confirm advice given through another Word of Knowledge. As you can see, the Word of Knowledge and physical healing often work hand-in-hand.

Occasionally I come across cases where physical healing is hindered by a spiritual condition. There are times when I have prayed for a person's healing and he or she was totally fine for three or four days, until suddenly the condition returned. I have also met people who have been prayed for hundreds of times regarding the same illness, but without ever receiving healing.

These cases raise questions. Questions are fine—the problem comes only when we try to answer those questions with our limited human logic. For instance, when a person has been prayed for so many times without results, some might say, "Well, I guess it just isn't God's will." The problem is that this so-called "answer" is born out of discouragement rather than the Word of God. Did the Holy Spirit specifically say that it was not God's will?

In some instances, we may never know the answers. But there are also situations where spiritual roots may need to be uncovered. In other words, God, in His wisdom, allowed a certain illness as a way of hinting at a person's spiritual condition.

For instance, I once knew a woman who was diagnosed with cancer in her womb. The doctors scheduled her for a hysterectomy within a matter of a few weeks. Our church prayed for her at length, but there were no results. However, a lack of results is not necessarily evidence of a lack of faith or a lack of God's will, so I kept seeking God for an answer.

I saw a vision in my mind of a black silhouette of a person (sort of a cartoon) with a white, fibrous mass in the location of the womb. The picture zoomed in, and I saw tentacles reaching out from the cancer and a word written on the main body of it: "bitterness."

I took the woman aside and shared the vision. As I did this, I received further insight through the Word of Knowledge and said, "I specifically feel like the bitterness is directed toward a prominent female in your life—like your mom or your sister. Does that make sense?"

"Not that I can think of," she replied; so I shrugged it off and excused it away as though it was probably just my imagination.

Three days later, however, she called me to say that she had prayed about what I said. "I realized I had bitterness toward both my mom and my sister, so I asked God's forgiveness. I feel a lot better now, so I'm hoping the tests come back negative tomorrow." Sure enough, the doctors couldn't find the slightest trace of cancer.

I didn't realize it at the time, but in hindsight, I can see the correlation between the woman's spiritual condition and her physical one. As she sowed seeds of bitterness against significant women in her life, she reaped the ramifications as an attack against her own womanhood. Not only that, but just as she was cursing the womb from which she was born, she was receiving a curse in her own womb.

Do not be deceived: God cannot be mocked. A man reaps what he sows. The one who sows to please his sinful nature, from that nature will reap destruction... (Galatians 6:7-8a).

"Sowing and reaping" is a spiritual law. Just as orange seeds grow orange trees and apple seeds grow apple trees, so a spiritual harvest will be directly related to the seeds sown. You can see, then, why this woman's physical condition was so closely related to her spiritual condition.

Does this mean that all women with cancer like this have bitterness toward their mothers and sisters? Not at all. And if you pray for such a woman and she is not healed, this also does not necessarily mean that there is a similar spiritual root.

Not all physical ailments have spiritual roots. That's why the Word of Knowledge is so vital. We must receive revelation from God. We need to have the humility to admit that we don't know why healing doesn't always happen. Since the Bible doesn't tell us why, we can't say for sure. And, of course, there's really no value in speculating. But if the Holy Spirit reveals what's happening in a specific case, then we can deal with the issue and have confidence that God will carry through on His end.

The Word of Knowledge Building Faith

One of the men who has mentored me in my life, Pastor Dan, occasionally demonstrates a special form of this gift. I've seen him stop in the middle of his sermon and say something like, "Pardon me for a moment, but I just had a quick pain in the lower left area of my back. Is there anyone here struggling with that same pain? I think the Lord wants to heal you." Sure enough, someone would raise their hand, he would pray, and God would bring the healing.

In this case, God used the Word of Knowledge to build faith. Speaking as someone who has been healed in this way myself, I know what a shift takes place in your mindset when someone calls out your exact condition without any prior knowledge. It builds a person's faith. After all, if God can supernaturally reveal my condition to someone, then He can heal it too!

This particular operation of the Word of Knowledge has become popular among the so-called "faith-healers" and tel-evangelists of today. In one sense, I love the fact that many people do indeed get healed as they watch these programs or visit these meetings. But I am also aware that many of those people are really only being healed by their own faith. It's unfortunate that the minister often gets the glory that should be going to Jesus.

I certainly won't judge every minister on television with a blanket accusation. But there are very likely certain cases where the person is merely listing diseases without actually having a Word of Knowledge. Even this, however, can activate people's faith and affect their healing, which brings credibility to the minister. And the bigger the audience, the more likely it is that someone is watching who has the condition being named.[1]

For this reason, I don't know how to classify this kind of a Word of Knowledge. In one sense, it could be called weak because it is so easily counterfeited and has led many people astray after false teachers. In another sense, however, it can be called strong because it does often result in genuine physical healings with little effort on the part of the minister.

Perhaps the best approach is to simply guard it. When we're practicing a Word of Knowledge meant to build someone's faith for healing, we need to be careful not to get caught up in the moment. We need to watch ourselves lest pride set in.

Many times, Jesus said, "Your faith has healed you." But never once did He say, "My Word of Knowledge healed you." I've actually heard ministers declare this from the pulpit— that their Word of Knowledge came from God, and when he or she spoke it out, it brought healing to the person. This mindset gets people looking at a man rather than God. It lacks humility and is contrary to the nature and example of Christ.

Instead, why not praise God for the healing and encourage the person that his or her faith was effective? We don't even need to point out that our Word of Knowledge was the catalyst to ignite that faith. What are we trying to gain? Let's walk in humility.

How This Form of the Word of Knowledge Works

As mentioned before, knowledge—in the biblical sense—is not about information but rather experience. So it's not so much that a person has suddenly received information that someone is sick. Instead, it comes more in the form of truly knowing.

In some cases, like with Pastor Dan, it may be that you share the same sensation. This can enhance your compassion and ignite your own faith to pray for someone's healing. When this happens, you "know" because you are experiencing the same pain or illness. As we saw in Chapter One, "Jesus knows all about our troubles."

In other cases, I know of people who experience a tingling sensation or intense internal heat through which God is making them aware of a particular part of their body. They then know that God wants to heal that part of someone else.

In still other cases, it may come in the form of a vision or dream. Sometimes, like the story of our waitress, Andrea, it's a picture of the condition itself. In other instances, you might see the healing taking place.

I know of ministers who will see a vision of a vague figure getting out of a wheelchair. Then they'll ask the Lord for more detail and start to see identifiable features—like a shirt color, hair style, etc. After asking for further detail, they'll receive a clear picture in their mind of what the person looks like—sometimes even the person's name. Upon arrival at a meeting or other destination, they'll look for that person and have the opportunity to be the vessel God uses to bring healing.

Responsibility and the Word of Knowledge

Be careful what you wish for, though. When you ask God for a Word of Knowledge regarding healing, realize that you're then responsible to carry out your part to administer that healing. If you don't, God won't condemn you, but you'll feel bad for not seizing the opportunity.

When I was first discovering this gift, I had not yet prayed for anyone regarding physical healing. But in my passion for the things of God, I really wanted it to happen and regularly asked the Lord for a gift of healing.

One day, our youth group had planned a trip to a Bavarian-themed city in Michigan called Frankenmuth. While I was praying over the trip—which would really only consist of shopping and eating—the Lord gave me a Word of Knowledge. I suddenly knew that I would come across a middle-aged woman in a wheelchair with short, black, curly hair.

In my naivety, I begged God, "OK, but please don't let her be a total paralytic who can only move her chair by blowing in a straw. I don't think I have the faith for that."

Sure enough, there I was sitting on the porch of a little candy shop when who should emerge from behind the next building but a middle-aged woman with short, black, curly hair—blowing in a straw to move her chair! Fear seized me. I argued with God. On one hand, I was convinced I didn't have enough faith. On the other hand, He had told me about this beforehand. I even considered the fact that I probably only thought about the "blowing in a straw" thing because God may have revealed that too.

I stood up. I sat down. I squirmed awkwardly. The woman and her family even stopped in front of the porch while her husband counted his money. My heart was pounding, and every excuse in the book was racing through my head. *I'm not ready for this. What makes me think I have a gift of healing? What if she doesn't get healed? Then what?*

As I battled inwardly with my fears and basic lack of compassion, the family moved on and I never saw the woman again. I felt worse having missed the opportunity than I would have felt if I had prayed without results. After the fact, I realized something: What was the worst that could have happened? Only that she might not get healed but would still learn that there are Christians who believe it can happen!

It's not that I still live with the regret—at least in the sense that I do not feel condemned or like a failure. But I do hold onto the feeling of heartache and remorse so I never forget the pain of missing an opportunity. Now, when the Lord speaks, it stirs me to act. If you receive a Word of Knowledge about someone's healing, step out and expect the results.

Summary Questions

1. How should we respond when people are not healed?

   _____

   _____

2. Describe how the spiritual law of sowing and reaping often affects people's physical condition, including their health.

   _____

   _____

3. Why is it that people can be healed even when someone fakes a Word of Knowledge?

   _____

   _____

4. Put yourself in my shoes during the last story I shared. How would you have responded when the woman in the wheelchair came around the corner? How should we respond to situations like these?

   _____

   _____

Endnote

1. Even in Jesus' ministry, people were often healed as a result of their own faith. So many times, Jesus would say, "Your faith has healed you." In the same way, people are often healed because their faith in God was activated through the Word of Knowledge or even a faked "Word of Knowledge." For examples of people being healed as a result of their own faith, see Matthew 9:22, Matthew 9:29, Mark 5:34, Luke 7:50, Luke 8:48, Luke 17:19, and Luke 18:42.

Chapter 5

the word of knowledge and intercession ↗

I hated my biology class. It was a cold winter morning in Michigan, and I was not in any way prepared for my final exam. Nevertheless, I drove to college to face my doom.

My heart was racing. I had struggled all semester to memorize all the information like our professor wanted. Not only that, but I got a few low scores on some projects, so I was already off to a rough start. And here I was on the day of the final exam with a blank mind. I couldn't remember anything. I was panicking. No matter how hard I tried, I couldn't meet my professor's high standards.

I pulled into my parking space ten minutes before class, which was great since it meant I had ten minutes to scramble through my textbook and hope to grab something of value.

God had different plans, though. As I got out of my car, a young lady got into the car in front of me and drove away. As soon as I saw her, the Holy Spirit gave me a Word of Knowledge. I suddenly knew that this young lady was about to face one of the most painful trials of her life, and I needed to pray for her.

It was sort of like when Jesus said to Simon Peter, "... *satan has asked to sift you as wheat. But I have prayed for you, Simon, that your faith may not fail...*" (Luke 22:31-32). How else would Jesus know this, apart from revelation from the Holy Spirit?

So there I was with a choice to make. I could use my ten minutes before class to cram for the most important exam of the semester, or I could pray for this young woman whom I had never met before, simply because I had an inkling in my spirit that she would need it soon.

I walked into class, sat down in my seat, and pushed my textbook aside. For the next ten minutes, I prayed silently for a total stranger. Through a Word of Knowledge, the Lord showed me someone who needed prayer and even prompted me how to pray.

I know what you're probably thinking: How do I know that I actually heard from God—especially since I never knew the young lady or ever saw her again? In one sense, I suppose I don't. However, the rest of the story seems to imply to me that God honored my actions—whether they were genuine obedience or merely an attempt.

I agonized through the test—guessing answers, writing paragraphs from my imagination, and doing everything I could to at least try to pass the test. Our professor gave everyone the option to wait in the hallway when we finished.

Then, one by one, he would call students back into the room to grade their test and give them their final score.

I was one of the last people to finish, so I sat in the hallway for some time. One by one, my classmates emerged from the room with looks of horror on their faces. Girls were crying. Guys were clenching their jaws and avoiding eye contact. One woman stepped out and sharply complained to her friend, "I can't believe I got a 'C!' I studied for days! That man doesn't know how to teach!"

Then came the moment of truth. My teacher poked his head out the door and flagged me in. I felt like I was walking to my execution. He lifted my test from the pile and dropped it unceremoniously onto the desk. His red pen flew down the first page and wrote a "20" at the bottom of the page—the same with the next two pages. Then came the essay questions. One question after the next, he wrote "5/5" without even reading the answers.

When I finally shook off the shock of what was happening, my conscience kicked into gear. "Umm…I actually didn't know the answer to that one…"

"Shh!" ordered my professor with a smirk.

He worked his way through the entire test, closed it, and wrote "4.0" at the top—for those who may not be familiar with this form of grading, a 4.0 is the highest score one can receive. Then he entered the score into his grade book and punched some numbers into his calculator.

"Looks like you're finishing the class with a 3.8. Is that what you were hoping for?"

"Wow...well..." I stammered, "This is more than I expected; but I, uh...I guess if you're asking what I was 'hoping' for, it would be a 4.0."

"Done."

My teacher wrote "4.0" in his grade book, shook my hand, and said, "Have a great break!"

I honestly didn't do anything to deserve this. I had not been a teacher's pet. The closest thing we had in common was our belief in a Creator; but he was Muslim, so it's not like we were chummy with our faith. To this day, I cannot figure out any earthly explanation for what took place that morning. The only thing that makes sense is that God was blessing me as a means of confirming that I had made the right decision to pray in response to the Holy Spirit.

Through a Word of Knowledge, the Holy Spirit can prompt you how to pray and what to pray. Jesus knows what is happening everywhere in the world, and at any given moment He may ask you to pray about something only He knows.

Revealing Strategic Details

Several years ago, I helped plant a church with Pastor Dan (whom I introduced in the previous chapter). One day, he and I drove out to a rural auto parts store to get what he needed to fix his daughter's truck. The place was huge and included a garage, a storage warehouse, and a salvage yard.

As soon as he and I walked into the front office, I felt like I had stepped into a spiritual steam room. The air felt thick and heavy—not physically, but spiritually. The atmosphere just felt uncomfortable in my spirit. It was as if something was sitting on my chest.

What I was experiencing in that moment would be best defined as "discerning spirits" because I was perceiving the spiritual environment. Not only that, but I could also discern that the spiritual environment I was sensing had something to do with sensuality and lust. These being two primary sins from which Christ has set me free, I tend to be particularly sensitive to them.

The guy took us into the warehouse to get the part needed. The deeper inside we got, the darker it felt.

On the way out, I asked the Holy Spirit what I had sensed. Through a Word of Knowledge, I suddenly knew that a pornography business was being run out of that building. In fact, I had the sense that it wasn't just being sold there but was actually being produced.

Getting into the car, I asked Pastor Dan, "Did you feel that in there?"

"Sure did. What do you think it was?"

"Well," I answered, "at first I was just sensing spiritual darkness, but then, I think I sensed something more specific…"

"Pornography. I know. I sensed it too," he responded, "And I think there was more going on there than just selling it…"

"They were producing it," I interjected.

"Exactly."

Armed with this very specific knowledge, we then knew exactly how to pray. Truth be told, we later regretted not going back into the building to confront the guy—after all, we had both sensed the exact same thing. But in the moment, all we felt led to do was pray, so perhaps that's all God wanted from us.

We prayed for the man who worked there. We prayed for his salvation. We prayed that the Holy Spirit would infiltrate that entire facility and convict everyone of their separation from God. Through the Word of Knowledge, the Holy Spirit revealed to us a very specific scenario that led us to pray accordingly. Had it not been for the Word of Knowledge, we would never have prayed.

As you can see, when the Word of Knowledge is used to prompt us how to pray, there often isn't much evidence to back up what we're sensing. In my experience, the most common scenario is simply that I feel prompted to pray about something specific, but I never truly know whether my prayer was of any effect, or whether the sense I had was indeed accurate.

Knowing What's Happening

The Holy Spirit can occasionally reveal what's happening as you pray. This use of the Word of Knowledge is tricky to define because it can easily be confused with the gift of Discerning Spirits.

Discerning Spirits has to do with perceiving and understanding activity in the spiritual realm—much like my experience at the auto parts warehouse. The Word of Knowledge, however, deals more with sensing things in the natural realm, including the human soul. Nevertheless, there are still certain instances when this gift enables us to "know" something spiritual.

For instance, consider how Jesus knew that satan wanted to sift Peter like wheat. This can be a little sketchy because on one hand, it could have been the gift of Discerning Spirits—Jesus may have had a vision in which He saw the conversation play out between His Father and satan. On the other hand, He may have suddenly simply known. In this case, it would have been a Word of Knowledge at work—suddenly having knowledge of spiritual reality.

Now and then, we find the lines blurring between spiritual gifts. That's why it's less important to figure out which gift is in operation at a given moment and more important to simply follow the Holy Spirit.

With this in mind, be aware that sometimes the Lord will enable you to know what is happening in spiritual warfare. Sometimes this will be through discerning spirits and other times through the Word of Knowledge. What matters is that we recognize these promptings and act on them.

Sometimes when I'm praying, the Lord will reveal to me what is happening in the spiritual realm, which serves to guide my focus and the development of my prayer. In one moment, I may be praying for someone to be convicted of sin. The next moment, I might feel that I need to start praying for that person to take action. When that seems settled, I may feel that it is necessary to pray for his or her safety. And after that, I may begin praying that the person's human spirit would be awakened to the voice of God. In each case, the reason I start praying about something new is because the Holy Spirit made known to me that either something was resolved or something else needed attention.

This interaction with the Holy Spirit will dramatically enhance your relationship with God. People often ask how it is that some Christians can spend hours in prayer without getting bored, daydreaming, or falling asleep. My best answer is that these Christians are typically interacting with God rather than delivering a monologue. When we listen for God's voice, He will direct our prayers. He will bring people and situations to our minds, and we can then respond according to how heavily the matter presses on our hearts. Our emotions, therefore, get involved, and God's will is prayed with passion.

Depending on your personal mix of spiritual gifts, your prayer time will differ from the next passionate believer. But all Christians have the capacity to hear God's voice in one form or another. One of those methods is through the Word of Knowledge, so people who have this gift should expect their gift to be in operation during times of prayer and intercession.

Knowing When Prayers Are Answered

Occasionally, the Word of Knowledge can help you to know when your prayers have been answered. Many intercessors often talk about praying until there is breakthrough. In essence, what they're talking about is continuing to pray until they sense—through a Word of Knowledge—that the prayer has been answered. Suddenly, there is an awareness that the time spent in prayer has been effective and there is no longer a need to pray about that subject.

This is particularly effective when you're praying from a distance. I once received a phone call from a friend of mine who was having a fight with her fiancé. I told her that I would pray for them, so I hung up the phone and fell to the ground in intercession. For almost a half-hour, I cried out to the Lord and pleaded for Him to send peace into the scenario. I wept for them. I spoke prophetic words toward them (even though they couldn't hear me). I basically did whatever the Holy Spirit was leading me to do.

Then, all of a sudden, I felt an unexplainable peace. I knew that the matter had been settled. I knew that God had answered. I knew that there was no sense continuing to pray.

I liken it to what happens when you ask someone to grab something for you from the other room. As soon as they get up and head to the other room, you know you don't need to ask anymore. You may not have the item in your hands, but you know that your request has been answered.

In the same way, the Word of Knowledge can make you aware that your request has been answered in the unseen realm. When there is no other way to know when to stop praying, the Holy Spirit can reveal the breakthrough.

Knowing What Not to Pray For

It is not uncommon for someone to come to me and ask me to pray, but often, as is the case with humanity at large, the prayer request is purely selfish or born from wrong motives. Sometimes it is glaringly obvious, and sometimes it is subtle. It's in these instances of subtleness that we need the Word of Knowledge.

I once had a gentleman come to me and say, "I need prayer for my marriage. My wife is causing a lot of grief between my children and me."

Before the first word came out of my mouth, the Lord gave a Word of Knowledge. It was as if everything inside of me screamed, "STOP!" So I paused. I closed my eyes. I asked the Lord for direction, and fuller detail came.

"You're correct that you need prayer for your marriage," I said, "but do you think it's possible that your wife really isn't causing any grief between you and your children?"

The man was silent. I tried to read his body language, but he wasn't giving me any signals.

"I am going to pray for your marriage, and I am going to pray for your relationship with your children," I said, "But I have a feeling that the grief between you and your children is your own fault. You need to be the loving father God created you to be. If that were taking place, then you would be above reproach and it wouldn't matter what your wife said."

116

Finally, the man broke. "You're right," he sighed, adjusting his stance to own up to his need for change. We prayed for only a couple of minutes, but he came back to me the next week to excitedly share how things had started shifting in his home life.

The Word of Knowledge is a great tool in prayer and intercession. Not only can it reveal what to pray, but it can save us from rambling unnecessarily about things that are not in accordance with God's will. (See 1 John 5:14.) Furthermore, it can be used to direct our times of prayer as the Holy Spirit makes known to us what Jesus Christ knows to be true in the moment.

Summary Questions

1. What is the difference between the Word of Knowledge and the gift of Discerning Spirits?

   _____

   _____

2. List some ways that the Word of Knowledge can enhance your times of prayer and intercession.

   _____

   _____

3. What should you do when you think you might have received a Word of Knowledge prompting you to pray

about something, but there is no evidence to prove that there actually is a need for prayer?

_____

_____

4. Take a moment to ask the Lord what He would like you to pray about. As thoughts, names, or images pop into your head, begin to pray for those situations. Don't be afraid to ask for more detail when the message seems unclear.

_____

_____

Chapter 6

the word of knowledge and evangelism ↗

It was Mother's Day, and I was in the middle of an hour-long drive between my church and my sister's house. I used to have a bad habit of leaving things until the last minute, so I knew at some point I would have to stop somewhere to pick up a card for my mom.

I thought about all the most ideal places along the route, and finally settled on a pharmacy right by my sister's home. It was a low-traffic area, and I would be able to get in and out quickly.

Nevertheless, God had His own plans. Four miles ahead was a Meijer—a huge store with almost every category of grocery, hardware, toys, tapestries, shoes, clothing, gifts, and, of course, cards. I knew it wouldn't be a quick entrance and exit, but for some reason this store was nagging my thoughts.

The Holy Spirit kept putting that store in my mind. I couldn't shake it.

"Why do you want me to waste my time at Meijer?" I asked in desperation.

Suddenly, I knew that when I walked into the store, I would be greeted by an elderly woman. I could sense her as if she were with me in the car right then.

"What am I supposed to do, Lord?" I asked.

Within my thoughts, the Lord replied, "Go buy a Mother's Day card for her, sign 'Jesus' on the inside, seal it, and give it to her."

Sure enough, as I walked into Meijer, there was the old woman I knew would be there, smiling and welcoming me to the store.

"Ugh," I thought, "I guess this means I'll have to go through with this!" It may seem strange to you that I was so reluctant, but put yourself in my shoes. What God was asking of me was sort of weird.

I went back to the card aisle and started scoping out the sparse selection that had already been picked over by many other last-minute shoppers. Impossible as it seemed to find a card that would work, I picked one up and read the verse. It was one of those cards that didn't really call the person "mom" but still affirmed her as a mother who had been faithful and loving. It included a prayer and words of thanksgiving for a life of sacrifice. It was beautifully written and seemed to fit the assignment perfectly, so I grabbed it.

Then I grabbed a funny cartoon card for my own mom. Aren't I a great son?

After check-out, I signed the card on the saddle of a mechanical horse and walked back to the door.

"Here," I said with a smile to the woman, "this is for you."

"What's this?" she inquired as she gently took the card from my hand.

"It's a Mother's Day card. This may sound strange to you, but God told me to buy this for you. Just consider it a blessing from Jesus."

Tears welled up in the old woman's eyes. "You don't know how special this is."

I was still pretty young and naïve at the time, so I didn't know what to do next. I felt a little awkward, but I muttered, "Well, God bless you!" and I shuffled out the door. Looking back, I should have asked the woman why it was so special and offered to pray with her, but I know she sensed God's love anyhow.

Pinpoint Targeting

The first way the Word of Knowledge comes in handy for evangelism is in finding prime subjects. Had it not been for the Word of Knowledge, I would have never thought to give a card to that woman. Not only that, but I can imagine that if I had come up with the idea on my own, I would have argued myself out of it by the time I reached the card aisle. I would have thought something like, "Well, if I buy her a card, then I have to buy one for every old woman in the store. What's so special about her?"

On the other hand, because of the Word of Knowledge, it was as if no one else existed. I had specific instructions from the Holy Spirit about who would greet me and what I should do. I found myself on a mission rather than waiting for an opportunity to arise by mere happenstance.

In general, we tend to have two natural mindsets when it comes to evangelism in America today. The first is "waiting," in which we go through life hoping a door will one day open wide enough for a semi truck to drive through. Unfortunately, this rarely happens; and since there's no risk involved, it doesn't really take any faith.

The second natural mindset is "saturation," in which our churches send out mass mailings in hopes that a few people will respond. Our "street evangelists" try to talk to everyone who gives them eye contact. We have door-hangers and gospel tracts galore. And people are encouraged to invite anyone they can to church services and events. There's nothing wrong with any of this—in fact if all our efforts only reached one person in the world, they would be worth it. Nevertheless, you have to admit that such methods are time consuming, costly, and have minimal effects when compared to the work put into them.

Imagine how much money our churches would save—and how much more effective they would be—if we relied on the Word of Knowledge. What if instead of 15,000 mailers, we printed only 500 invitations, placed them in the hands of passionate believers, and commissioned them to seek the Holy

Spirit for direction before giving them out? What would happen if all those believers received a Word of Knowledge about whom to invite? Do you think we would be more or less effective than the money spent on a mass mailing?

Let me step back off my soapbox for a moment and reiterate that mailings aren't bad. My objective is simply to point out the effectiveness of the Word of Knowledge. Through this spiritual gift, we can be directed to specific people who are ready to make a decision for Christ. It is true that "the fields are white for the harvest," but not everyone is ready to make a decision for Christ. The Word of Knowledge helps us "to seek and to save what was lost." (See Luke 19:10.)

Treasure Hunting

Pastor Kevin Dedmon from Bethel Church in Redding, California, wrote a book titled *The Ultimate Treasure Hunt.*[1] In it, he focuses on how simple pieces of information can be gathered through the Word of Knowledge and then used to find specific people whom God is highlighting for an encounter. Basically, he takes a team of believers and has them ask God for "clues." Then they write down the words or pictures that come to mind—fitting them into categories of places, attributes, ailments, and so forth.

Armed with these "Treasure Maps," the teams head out to the public in search of human-treasure. There they share the Gospel, pray for healing, prophesy, and otherwise share the love of God with people. Dedmon's book is filled with one testimony after another of supernatural encounters that were only possible because ordinary people acted on a simple list of clues that were born out of the Word of Knowledge.

My wife Robin and I recently took two teens from our youth group and one of our church's interns out on a Treasure Hunt. We got our team together, watched a short video of some other "Treasure Hunters," and set to work.

The five of us spent a few minutes asking the Holy Spirit to speak to us and point us to people who specifically needed a touch from Him. Each of us wrote down random clues as they popped into our minds, and then we compared notes at the end.

One person had a vision of "roller skates," and another wrote down "Meijer." We live in the Detroit Metropolitan area, and there are five Meijer stores within twenty minutes of our church. But the "roller skates" clue pointed us to the only Meijer near a Sonic restaurant (where the carhops wear "roller skates"). As if to confirm to us that we were in the right location, next door to the Meijer was a large clock that was built into the architecture of a vacant building, which one of the teens had seen in a vision and written down. The clues were all lining up with what the Holy Spirit had prompted our group to write! We were certain that we were on the hunt for something real!

Since someone had written down "bakery" and "red and blue balloons," we thought a good place to start would be in the bakery next to a cake with red and blue balloons on it. It didn't take more than a couple minutes before a girl we'll call "Abby" came walking by.

Abby matched clues from several of our lists: "long hair," "big sunglasses," and "pregnant." Robin and one of our teens approached her and started a conversation. As it turned out, she matched more clues than those that were obvious. In conversation, Robin and the teen learned that a week before finding out she was pregnant, Abby had been diagnosed with cancer. "Cancer" was also on one of our lists, and so was "Right leg," which happened to be where she was having another related problem.

Robin and the teen prayed for Abby's healing and the health of her baby, and then we moved on.

We searched the store, following clues from one end to the other. I talked to one older gentleman with really no results and was a little discouraged that I hadn't gotten to pray with anyone yet. Our little adventure was happening prior to a youth service I was helping to lead, so we were quickly running out of time. Eventually, we decided we should probably head back to the church.

On our way to the front of the store, though, we spotted a young lady in a brown hoodie, which someone had written down. Two people from our group walked down that aisle to ask if she needed prayer, and the rest of us moved to the next aisle where I saw an older woman limping as she pushed her cart.

The woman with the limp didn't match any of the clues on our lists (except possibly "right leg"), but I knew the opportunity was too good to pass up, so we started down the aisle to pray with her. By the time we got there, the young lady in the brown hoodie walked around the corner. As it turns out, it was the limping woman's daughter. The rest of our group came around also, and now we were all packed into the little aisle.

"Excuse me," I said to the woman, "I couldn't help but notice you were limping. Do you mind if I ask what happened?"

"Yeah—I have really bad arthritis in both my knees, and it's hard to walk."

"Well," I replied, "I'll just be honest with you. We're here this afternoon looking for people to pray for, so do you mind if we pray for you real quick?"

"Oh, um, sure," she answered.

With her permission, I placed my hand on her shoulder and prayed a simple, 10-second prayer, thanking God for His love and asking Him to heal her knees in the name of Jesus.

"Amen." That was it. "Do you feel any different?" I asked.

The woman shuffled back and forth and said, "Actually, it's a little bit better."

"Awesome," I responded, "That means it's working! Do you mind if we pray again?"

The woman smiled, "I guess not."

Again we prayed. "How is it now? See if you can do something you couldn't do before."

The woman started to march in place, bending her knees with a look of shock on her face. "I couldn't do that before," said the woman. "It barely hurts at all now, and that says a lot since I could barely walk before. I have no cartilage in either knee, so it usually hurts a lot."

"Sweet! Then let's pray that God would cause new cartilage to grow!"

"You can do that?" she asked, a little hesitant.

"Sure; it happens all the time when people pray. Do you mind if we pray one more time?"

Apparently our faith was a little too much for the woman to handle. "Uh, I think I'm good," she said, and she quickly walked away...but she walked!

The rest of our group said goodbye warmly, and we headed back to the church for that night's youth meeting.

On the way back, we looked over all our "clues" that had brought us to these divine encounters, and we were shocked to see how many had been actively involved in leading us to these "Treasures." A handful of people—most of whom had never practiced the spiritual gift of a Word of Knowledge— listened to the Holy Spirit and wrote down words that they weren't even sure would mean anything. What a leap of faith—especially for the teens who had never done anything like this before!

I began to think about how much more effective we were than any other time I had gone out trying to share the Gospel with random people. Rather than going for just anyone at all, we set out after people who were being specifically targeted by God!

Knowing the Person

A number of years ago, I had a small group that met in my girlfriend (now wife) Robin's home. It was an interdenominational fellowship in which we loved Christ and one another, studied the Word of God, and discovered the miraculous power of the Holy Spirit through prayer and evangelism. Those who joined our group as skeptics against spiritual gifts soon found themselves practicing them. In fact, it was the Word of Knowledge that got the ball rolling and opened our skeptical friends' eyes to what was possible through the Holy Spirit.

Robin's dad received a phone call one afternoon from a friend on the other side of the state who was a pastor. He shared about a young man from his hometown who was living near us and needed some godly support in a decision he was making. Robin's dad immediately recommended our small group.

The next Monday, in walked Philip. He was neatly dressed, clean-shaven, and looked like he might be in his first year of college. Naturally, our group welcomed him with open arms and started to ask him about himself.

Philip seemed to be beating around the bush in those opening minutes, but things changed when the time came to officially start.

"Is everyone here now?" he asked.

"I think so," I replied.

"Good. Do you mind if I share my story?"

For the next few minutes, Philip told us how he ended up at our meeting. He said he had never really been a Christian, but when he was a teenager, there was a pastor and his wife down the street who always tried to talk to him—this was the man who had called Robin's dad.

After about five minutes of nervously sharing his history, Philip blurted out a confession.

"What you guys have to know about me is…" Philip paused for a moment and looked me in the eye, "I'm gay."

To be honest, I wasn't shocked by that comment. I was more concerned with hoping the rest of our group would respond like Jesus. There were no audible gasps, and I was proud of our little church.

Realizing he wasn't being judged, Philip continued to pour out his story with tears. In short, he was living in a relationship with a man in the area and suddenly had a realization that his lifestyle wasn't right. Philip wanted out, and the only person he knew to call was that pastor and his wife back home.

There we sat. I had never encountered a situation like this before. On the outside, I was completely calm and collected. On the inside, I was begging God for insight so that I could say exactly the right thing.

Then Philip said, "I know the Bible says homosexuality is bad, but isn't there a gay gene? Why would God make me gay if it's a sin?"

The Holy Spirit rose up within me and I had an answer that I had never formulated before. We could probably define it as a gift of a Word of Wisdom because the Holy Spirit took wisdom from Christ and made it supernaturally known to me.

I simply replied, "It is true that scientists have found a piece in the genetic code that seems to make people more or less prone toward homosexuality. However, it's no different than the fact that they have found genes that make people more or less prone to outbursts of anger, alcoholism, and so forth.

"God has a purpose for everyone. When He creates us, He gives us exactly the DNA that can help us succeed in bringing the most glory to Him.

"Suppose He creates one person to be a fiery, bold, passionate speaker of the Truth who isn't afraid to share the Gospel with anyone. But then the enemy comes along, reads the DNA, and says, 'Ah ha! I'll twist this plan and try to give this person a problem with rage.' The enemy pulls out all the stops to manipulate circumstances and pervert the plan of God. And unless the person is on guard, he will very likely default to the plan of the enemy because we are born into lives of separation from God.

"Rage is sin. The Bible doesn't say that 'fits of rage' are sinful, except when they're the result of your DNA. Rage is sin, period. One of the reasons it is sin is because 'fits of rage' was not God's original intent when He wove that DNA together at conception. Instead, He intended something that could be beneficial and powerful for the person to live a fulfilled life as part of His Kingdom."

Yes, all that came as one sudden download from Heaven—sort of in a mashed-up ball rather than a string of words. I articulated the thoughts on the fly as I spoke. And when I had finally worked my way to the end, the Holy Spirit brought a Word of Knowledge that would help me apply all this to Philip.

I suddenly knew Philip as if we had been friends for years—as though I had been present when God planned his destiny and purpose for this world. I spoke gently to him as the Spirit led.

"Philip," I began, "God created you as a compassionate, tender-hearted person who regularly makes sacrifices to be a good friend to anyone who needs one. Am I right?"

Philip nodded in astonishment.

"The enemy, however, saw the potential that God wrote into your DNA and said, 'I'm going to twist that destiny and stir up homosexual thoughts and feelings.' Since you weren't serving God, you were more focused on gratifying your own desires than fulfilling your purpose, which is why you walked down the path that you did."

Philip later testified that it was as if his whole life suddenly made sense. We prayed with him to receive salvation and proceeded with our meeting.

At the end, we started a time of prayer, and Philip asked us to pray that he could find a new place to live so he could get out of his current living situation. One of the men from our small group invited him to come live with him and his wife for a few weeks, and Philip accepted.

Another person felt led to give him a particular amount of money. When Philip drove out onto the road that night after our small group, he was immediately pulled over for having a burnt-out taillight. The money he received was exactly what he needed to buy a new one.

Why do I share these extra details? Because I want you to know that all the gifts of the Spirit are necessary in the Church! The Word of Knowledge gave me insight into Philip's life, but I wouldn't have known what to do with it had it not been for the Word of Wisdom I received just before. Then we have to wonder what might have happened to Philip if a couple from our group hadn't exercised the Gift of Hospitality by taking him in. Philip would have had to stay that night with the man he was leaving—clearly an unhealthy environment. And what about the Gift of Giving that was expressed? Without that, Philip would have had one more stress to distract him from his newfound life. Instead, Philip had yet another proof that God cares deeply about him—regardless of his history.

Philip's life changed dramatically. In the coming months, we walked through the healing of wounds in his heart, the discovery of biblical truth, and the battling of temptation. Philip grew quickly in his new life, was filled with the Holy Spirit, and began to demonstrate the Gift of Prophecy and the Word of Knowledge himself. He regularly looked for opportunities to share the Gospel with new people. Philip was a dramatically different person, all because he encountered God—first through the inner conviction of the Holy Spirit, second through a family of believers who were actively practicing gifts of the Spirit, and thirdly (and most importantly) through a personal experience with the life-transforming death and resurrection of Jesus Christ.

The Word of Knowledge was just one part of that process, but it was an essential part. Through a Word of Knowledge, God can give you insights into the life of a person even when you have never previously met. It is then our own responsibility to use that knowledge appropriately and apply it as the Holy Spirit leads.

Shocking the İntellect

There is no doubt that God has used "shock and awe" tactics throughout history to get people's attention. Consider the "burning bush" episode with Moses. Did God really have to show up as a blazing bush in the desert? Of course not—He could have spoken with a "still small voice" like He did to Elijah. (See 1 Kings 19:12.) But God knew that He needed to get Moses' attention in a dramatic way if He would convince the humble sheepherder to leave his steady night job and go confront the Pharaoh!

Occasionally, God uses the Word of Knowledge in this same way—to get attention from people who wouldn't otherwise believe. It is true that many people come to Christ without any supernatural experience taking place around them, but I wonder if that is God's sovereign decision or if it is actually our own fault as the Church. Imagine how many more people would come to faith after supernatural encounters if more Christians were out in the world ushering those encounters into reality. I believe it is possible, and the Word of Knowledge is one of the tools at our disposal.

The sun was high in its arch, and Jesus' disciples were in the nearby city buying lunch. Meanwhile, Jesus had a seat by a local well to recharge from His journey. About 2,400 years earlier, one of Jesus' ancestors, Jacob, had purchased that land and had dug that well. But now the land was in the possession of Samaritans—people of mixed descent who were generally shunned by the pureblooded Jews. Jesus and His disciples had to pass through the town on their way to Galilee, and now He was thirsty as the noonday sun blazed overhead.

It didn't take long before a Samaritan woman came to the well to draw water. Jesus broke the silence by asking for a drink from the bucket she pulled up.

The woman was confused. Jews didn't talk to Samaritans, and men of that culture didn't address women—especially strangers. One might think that this would be enough to shock her into realizing there was something different about this man, but she responded in a natural way: *"How come you, a Jew, are asking me, a Samaritan woman, for a drink?"* (John 4:9 MSG).

Jesus pushed a little further, trying to move things to a more spiritual conversation.

Jesus replied, "If you only knew the gift God has for you and who you are speaking to, you would ask me, and I would give you living water."

"But sir, you don't have a rope or a bucket," she said, "and this well is very deep. Where would you get this living water? And besides, do you think you're greater than our ancestor Jacob, who gave us this well? How can you offer better water than he and his sons and his animals enjoyed?"

Jesus replied, "Anyone who drinks this water will soon become thirsty again. But those who drink the water I give will never be thirsty again. It becomes a fresh, bubbling spring within them, giving them eternal life."

"Please, sir," the woman said, "give me this water! Then I'll never be thirsty again, and I won't have to come here to get water" (John 4:10-15 NLT).

So far, Jesus has said three things that should have shaken the woman out of her natural mindset. First, the mere fact that He spoke to her—a Samaritan, and a woman at that—should have given her a clue that this was no ordinary Jewish guy. Second, He revealed that He has some sort of spiritual life to offer as a gift from God, but it breezed right past her as she couldn't figure out how He was going to get this "water" without a rope or bucket. Third, Jesus describes this "living water" and the fact that it results in eternal life.

In my mind, I imagine the woman finally putting one hand on her hip and throwing the other in the air as she says, "Well, then, since you're so insistent, let's have it! Give me some of this water!"

All three statements were enough to get a rise out of the woman, but none of them brought her into a spiritual mindset. None of Jesus' statements penetrated her heart. As

First Corinthians 4:20 says, *"For the kingdom of God is not a matter of talk but of power."* It was about time for Jesus to move beyond spiritual talk and demonstrate spiritual power. Maybe that would trigger the woman's heart to respond in the right way.

"Tell you what," He said, "Go get your husband, bring him back here, and then we'll get back to this 'living water' thing."

"But I don't have a husband," she replied.

"That's true," Jesus answered. "Actually, you've had five husbands, and you're not married to the man you're living with now."

Finally, the woman's spirituality came awake. "You must be a prophet!" she exclaimed. What followed was a genuine spiritual conversation. But it wasn't their conversation about living water or their later conversation of worship that gripped this woman with excitement. Instead, she left her water jar there by the well and ran to all her neighbors declaring, *"Come and meet a man who told me everything I ever did! Can this be the Messiah?"* (John 4:29 NLT).

I find that really interesting since Jesus outright said in verse 26 that He was indeed the Messiah! This woman made no mention of the living water or the conversation about worship. What sparked her enthusiasm was the fact that Jesus had a Word of Knowledge.

Sometimes all the words in the world seem to fall on deaf ears when we're trying to share the Gospel. That's when power-encounters like healing, prophecy, and the Word of Knowledge come in handy. Like the burning bush God used to grab the attention of Moses, these demonstrations of God's love and power capture attention and snap people to life. The Word of Knowledge can be a powerful tool in evangelism.

Summary Questions

1. How can a Word of Knowledge make us more effective at reaching people who are ready to make a decision for Christ?

_____

_____

2. How can a Word of Knowledge help us when we are ministering to someone we have never previously met?

_____

_____

3. What is it about a Word of Knowledge that seems to make it such an effective tool in evangelism?

_____

_____

4. Find a friend and go on a "treasure hunt." Start with prayer, write down the "clues" that come to mind (related to locations, names, a person's appearance, what

they might need prayer for, and any other random or unusual thoughts). Follow the clues and look for people who might be on the list. Strike up a conversation with those people and see where it takes you! Try to spend more time asking the person questions and listening to their answers than you spend telling them things. Ask to pray, and expect results!

Endnote

1.   Kevin Dedmon (2007). *The ultimate treasure hunt: a guide to supernatural evangelism through supernatural encounters.* Shippensburg, PA: Destiny Image Publishers, Inc.

Chapter 7

the word of knowledge at work in ministry ↗

Two thousand dollars went missing. The church fundraiser money was gone, and our youth mission trip to Mexico was in jeopardy.

I was particularly bothered—but not for noble reasons. I had spent extra money to have my passport rush-delivered, and this would mean I had spent all that money for nothing!

In my disgust over what had happened, the Holy Spirit finally convicted me. I was just as guilty of sin as whoever stole the money because I was more upset about the loss from my own bank account than the lost people of Mexico.

With reluctant yet willful repentance, I turned my focus to what God wanted to do. I began to pray for God to "reveal what is hidden" and help us recover the missing money. Little did I know how He would go about answering. As I sought God, the Holy Spirit gave me a Word of Knowledge about who had taken the money and how they had already spent most of it.

To be honest, the first thing that crossed my mind was the story of Ananias and Sapphira from the fifth chapter of Acts. This couple sold a piece of land, brought some of the money to the apostles, and withheld the rest of it. That action in itself doesn't appear to be the problem. The real issue was that they lied by saying that the money they were giving to the apostles was everything they had received from the sale.

I can only imagine being in Peter's shoes. He had received a Word of Knowledge about what had actually taken place. Peter knew in his spirit that Ananias and Sapphira had lied about their giving. What would I have done in his situation?

Many of us would be tempted to let something like this just get swept under the rug. After all, no one was hurt, and they did give some money. Who cares if they kept a little for themselves?

Wait a minute. That's not entirely true. Someone did get hurt. Can you guess who? Peter's focus was not on himself or even the church—in fact, it wasn't even on Ananias and Sapphira. Peter's focus was on the One he loved.

Then Peter said, "Ananias, why has Satan filled your heart? You lied to the Holy Spirit, and you kept some of the money for yourself. The property was yours to sell or not sell, as you wished. And after selling it, the money was yours to give away. How could you do a thing like this? You weren't lying to us but to God" (Acts 5:3-4 NLT).

Given the way things tend to happen in today's world (at least in America), most of us would probably be shocked simply at Peter's words to Ananias. But what happened next would be utterly unthinkable. As soon as Peter finished his rebuke, Ananias fell down dead! And no, he wasn't resurrected. Instead, some young men wrapped him up in a sheet and buried him in the back yard.

About three hours later his wife came in, not knowing what had happened. Peter asked her, "Was this the price you and your husband received for your land?"

"Yes," she replied, "that was the price."

And Peter said, "How could the two of you even think of doing a thing like this—conspiring together to test the Spirit of the Lord? Just outside that door are the young men who buried your husband, and they will carry you out, too."

Instantly, she fell to the floor and died. When the young men came in and saw that she was dead, they carried her out and buried her beside her husband (Acts 5:7-10 NLT).

I began to picture this story playing out with the two young people from my youth group whom I saw in my vision. My heart was grieved over the way they had stolen from the Lord. That was the Holy Spirit's money, and they had used it to feed their own addictions. I knew I had to confront them, but I couldn't face the possibility that they might be struck dead.

Suddenly, compassion gripped me. Perhaps nothing would have actually happened, but my fear of the Lord drove me to intercession. I began to plead for their lives. Since they were members of my youth group, I had a responsibility for their souls. I began to understand the heart of Christ as He laid down His own life for sinners.

Being armed with the Word of Knowledge isn't enough—we need to know God's heart. What does He want to do in the situation? Just because we know information doesn't mean we know the prescribed action. That's why it's so important to discover the heart of God through prayer.

That Sunday at church, I finished leading worship and closed by addressing the congregation:

"As many of you know, our youth group has been raising money to go to Mexico to work with an orphanage and share the Gospel."

Everyone clapped and cheered.

"Unfortunately, we just found out this week that about $2,000 worth of fundraiser money has been stolen."

Jaws dropped. People looked at each other in disbelief.

"I do know who took it…" I briefly looked the two young people in the eye—just long enough to see them gulp. I continued, "…and I know that they've already spent most of the money. I prayed a lot about how to respond, and I want those students to know that I forgive you.

"There is a price that needs to be paid, though. Without the $2,000, we cannot go to Mexico. I want to demonstrate to you what Jesus did for you. You don't deserve salvation, but Jesus paid the price for your freedom with his own life. In a similar way, even though you don't deserve it, I'm going to try to come up with the $2,000 myself and pay it out of my own pocket. I'm not going to call you out or ask for the money. It is paid in full.

"But know this: even though Jesus paid the price for your sin in full, you won't get to experience the benefit unless you make Him Lord of your life. You can't experience the benefit of my gift unless you realize that you don't need to pay back the $2,000, and you can't experience the benefit of Christ's gift unless you stop living for yourself. That involves repentance, which means putting your life of sin to death. I hope this example of Christ is enough to convince you that His blood can cover your sin and spare you from hell. I can save you from that $2,000, but only Jesus Christ can save you from eternal hell."

Those two young people sat silently through the entire meeting (not chatting like normal). They never came forward to confess their sin, but many of those in attendance later testified that what took place that morning transformed their understanding of Christianity. We also had several visitors that week, and a couple of them received salvation—one of whom we later found out was a witch who was so moved by this demonstration of the Gospel that she gave her life to Christ and started bringing her whole family to our church!

In this particular situation, the Word of Knowledge wasn't specifically given so that a couple sinners would be called out. Rather, it was given to shake me out of my selfish mindset and move me to compassion. The result was multiplication of the Kingdom as Jesus Christ was revealed in a practical way.

This is absolutely essential for ministry. Remember what we said in chapter one—the Word of Knowledge is not merely about receiving information. Rather, it is about truly knowing something God knows through revelation of the Holy Spirit.

I didn't just get the information about who had committed the crime—I understood the heart of Jesus as though these two young people were my own children. I saw that they were lost and had never come to a saving knowledge of Jesus Christ, and this moved me to action.

The Word of Knowledge can be very useful in ministry. It helps us minister God's grace and authority with power in appropriate ways. Consider Jesus' own ministry:

They came to Capernaum. When he was in the house, [Jesus] asked them, "What were you arguing about on the road?" But they kept quiet because on the way they had argued about who was the greatest.

Sitting down, Jesus called the Twelve and said, "If anyone wants to be first, he must be the very last, and the servant of all" (Mark 9:33-35).

The disciples knew they had done wrong by having that conversation. It's no wonder they didn't want to admit it to Jesus! But through a Word of Knowledge, Jesus knew exactly what message they needed to hear. He pinpointed the condition of their hearts and spoke directly to the issue.

The Word of Knowledge can give a preacher insight into the hearts and minds of his congregation. It can give the street-evangelist insight into the hearts and minds of those who need to hear the Gospel. It can give the counselor insight into the hearts and minds of counselees. The list could go on. Whatever your ministry, a spiritual gift of a Word of Knowledge can help enhance your effectiveness. It's not just because you are given extra information but also because you gain insight into God's will and heart through the Holy Spirit.

The Word of Knowledge and Christian Counseling

A young lady had requested counseling for her struggle with an eating disorder, so I called my pastor's wife and set up an appointment with the three of us. As I prepared for our time of ministry, I asked the Holy Spirit to reveal the root of her condition. Sure enough, He made known the mystery through a Word of Knowledge. I knew without doubt that the reason she was struggling with this particular eating disorder was because of bitterness she was holding in her heart against her mother.

The first commandment with a promise attached to it is "Honor your father and mother that it may go well with you and that you may enjoy long life on the earth." (See Ephesians 6:1-3.) What many people don't realize is that the opposite is also true: Dishonor your father and mother, and you will live a short life on the earth that does not go well with you. This is spiritual law. This young lady had dishonored her mother with bitterness; and because she had not yet surrendered that issue to the cross of Christ, spiritual law was working against her.

I didn't really know the woman that well at the time—and I had never met her mother—but Jesus knew them both. Knowing where we needed to head, I organized a series of questions to gently lead up to this matter of forgiving her mother.

It is important that we don't use the Word of Knowledge to pounce on people with condemnation or accusation. Even Peter gave Ananias and Sapphira one more chance to tell the truth without implying that he knew anything at all. Many people misuse the Word of Knowledge, assuming that it is just God's form of gossip. This couldn't be farther from the truth. The Word of Knowledge is Jesus—the Head of the Church—sending information and action steps to part of His Body. We can submit ourselves to the will of our Head, or we can spasm. One option heals, and the other wounds. If the Holy Spirit is revealing something to you, then you need to ask Him how Jesus wants you to use the information.

Imagine yourself kneeling in the middle of a battlefield. Before you is a mortally wounded soldier, and beside you is a medic who believes the man can be saved. Every second counts. The medic hands you a tool from his bag that you have never seen before. You have a few options. One possibility is that you could start beating the person with it, but that's definitely not how it should be used. On the other hand, you could try figuring out how to use it according to your own limited knowledge. Then again, there's the third option that you could ask the medic what he wants you to do. Which one is more likely to save the victim?

Sure enough, through the time of counseling, we uncovered that the woman really did have bitterness against her mother. But even after I had gently shared about spiritual law, God's love, and the forgiveness of Christ, she still refused to forgive her mother.

It is important that we don't use the Word of Knowledge like a battering ram. I could have pushed this young lady by saying, "Listen, the Holy Spirit revealed what your problem is, so it's obvious that it's time to deal with it. Get over your fear and just forgive your mother!" But this is what author, counselor, and teacher John Loren Sandford would call "emotional rape"—forcing a person to be vulnerable and personal when he or she truly doesn't want to.[1] I had to simply pray for the young woman and release her to contemplate what we discussed.

The Word of Knowledge can also be used to understand what is happening in the thought processes of counselees. After a small group meeting one night, everyone decided we would like to go out to eat at a nearby restaurant. A strange thing happened on the way out the door, though. One of the men who had been particularly vulnerable in the group that night, Jim, took a couple steps out the door and then bolted for his car.

I ran out into the street just in time to stop him from putting his car in drive after backing out. Jim rolled down his window as I walked to the side of his car, but he continued to stare blankly straight forward.

"What's happening, Jim?" I asked.

"I'm not going to the restaurant," came the stone-faced reply.

"Why not?" I pressed.

"I don't know."

"Well, Jesus does know. It looks like you feel embarrassed about what you shared tonight—even though we all supported you—and you're having a hard time accepting the fact that you really are accepted as part of this family."

Jim's eyes widened, and his head slowly turned toward me. He recognized that this was a Word of Knowledge.

We had a healthy conversation for the next few minutes that basically led Jim to the realization that his struggle wasn't just with the people of the group. In reality, he was having a hard time seeing himself as part of our spiritual family because he couldn't handle the idea that he was accepted by His spiritual Father in Heaven.

I began to prophesy to Jim about how much God loved him. While I was still speaking, I had another Word of Knowledge—I knew Jim's thoughts. I could hear him saying to God, "No You don't. You don't really love me like that. Look at all my problems..."

"Why are you arguing with God, Jim?" I asked. Jim's eyes snapped back to mine, and his breathing got heavier. "He loves you. Why would you argue with God? He loves you! He loves you enough to show me what's going on inside your head so I can prove that He's listening to you."

Jim's countenance changed and he started to laugh. He finally believed it and agreed to join us at the restaurant. Later that night, Jim testified that he couldn't believe God cared enough about him to actually listen to his thoughts. That one Word of Knowledge helped Jim receive God's Fatherly love and trust his spiritual family. The Word of Knowledge can be used powerfully in Christian counseling to uproot the deep issues and wounds of the heart so that healing can be applied through the cross of Christ.

The Word of Knowledge and Ministry to New People

In ministry, we come across new people all the time. Whether they come to us or we go to them, the fact remains that they have a history about which we know nothing. We don't know their wounds. We don't know how they have been abused and mistreated. We don't know how they were raised, how they are presently living their lives, or what manner of battles are taking place in their minds. We don't know their deepest felt needs.

The good news, however, is that Jesus does know their history, their thoughts, and their struggles. He knows everything about them. And through the Word of Knowledge, the Holy Spirit can make known to us what Jesus knows. We can receive insight into the most hidden corners of a person's heart and mind even without ever having met him.

The crowd was pressing in on all sides. The house was packed—people were crammed in the doorway and stretching through the windows to hear Jesus speak. If they had fire codes back then, the marshal would have surely shut them down.

Down the street was a man we'll call Frank. Frank was paralyzed and wouldn't have been able to get to Jesus if he wanted to. But Frank had some friends who knew about Jesus' power to heal. They came to Frank, grabbed the corners of his mat, and carried him off toward Jesus.

The Bible doesn't say so, but I get the feeling Frank didn't really want to go see Jesus. Based on what happened next, I get the impression that Frank was probably thinking something like: "I don't deserve to get healed—look at everything I've done wrong. There are plenty of people who have lived better lives than me. Why waste Jesus' time with such a sinful wretch? I deserve to die like this."

But Frank was paralyzed, so what was he going to do to stop them?

Shuffling up to the house, the four men bit their bottom lips and craned their necks to find a way inside.

Some say necessity is the mother of invention. These men had carried their friend down there to be healed by Jesus, and they weren't about to carry him back. I don't know who came up with the creative idea first, but it was probably someone like me—someone who was out of breath and thinking, "Seriously, Frank, this is the last time I'm lugging you around. I'm not in good enough shape for this!"

Whatever the case, when the four corners finally dropped from around Frank, he didn't see Jesus. Actually, he didn't even see all the people he was hearing. All he saw was open sky and his four friends digging a hole next to him.

Meanwhile, inside the house, Jesus was just getting to the third point of His sermon when a little waterfall of dirt and dust poured onto the floor in front of Him. Jesus paused and looked up just in time to see daylight piercing through the ceiling.

Fingers from several hands poked through the hole in the clay ceiling and pulled chunks away quickly. As the house filled with a cloud of dust, the circle of daylight overhead grew bigger and bigger.

Jesus waited patiently. There was no sense trying to continue preaching.

Suddenly, like an eclipse, the room grew dark again. Something had been moved to cover up the hole. And then, that "something" started to come through the hole! Light burst into the room once again as a package was lowered with ropes right down to the feet of Jesus.

When the cloth parcel hit the floor, the four corners lowered to reveal none other than Frank the paralytic. The whole crowd stood in stunned silence, waiting to see what Jesus would do.

At this point, I am convinced that Jesus had a Word of Knowledge. Think about it. Jesus was known all over the countryside for healing people, and now a paralyzed man was staring up at Him from the floor. The logical reaction would have been for Jesus to take the man by the hand and heal him. That's what everyone expected Him to do.

Jesus didn't heal him. He knew the more important first problem. Even though Jesus had never met Frank before, the Holy Spirit revealed his most pressing felt need.

Jesus broke the silence by saying, "Son, your sins are forgiven."

Now some teachers of the law were sitting there,
thinking to themselves, "Why does this fellow talk like

that? He's blaspheming! Who can forgive sins but God alone?"

Immediately Jesus knew in his spirit that this was what they were thinking in their hearts, and he said to them, "Why are you thinking these things?" (Mark 2:6-8).

Jesus was receiving Words of Knowledge left and right! I love the fact that no one else said a word. Only one voice filled the dusty air. Only one voice escaped through the hole in the roof. First, Jesus looked at the man and said, "Your sins are forgiven." Then He looked at the crowd and asked, "Why are you thinking these things?"

The silence continued—broken only by the uncomfortable shifting of weight in the crowd.

Jesus continued, "Wouldn't you say it's easier for me to tell this man, 'Your sins are forgiven,' than it would be for me to say, 'Get up and walk!'?"

The crowd still stared in shock over everything that was taking place, but in their minds, they knew Jesus' logic was correct. It was indeed an easier thing to say.

"Well then, how about I say the more difficult thing so that you will know that the son of man has authority on earth to forgive sin."

Jesus looked Frank in the eye and smiled. "Get up," He said, "take your mat, and go home."

The four friends' heads loomed over the sides of the hole above, and they watched as Frank slowly stood to his feet, rolled up his mat, and took his first steps. The formerly impenetrable crowd now parted like the Red Sea, and Frank went home.

The four friends let out a sigh, relieved that they didn't have to hoist Frank back up through the roof. Then they high-fived each other and ran away before the owner of the house had a chance to bill them for the damages. (OK, I made that last part up.)

The Word of Knowledge can help us know exactly how to minister to people even when their physical circumstances are jockeying for our attention. In ministry, you will regularly come across total strangers who have a very visible need. Many times, however, if their deeper need isn't dealt with first, they will have a hard time sensing God's love through even the most amazing miracle. The Word of Knowledge can help make that need known.

The Word of Knowledge and Pastoring People

Let's go back to the couple with the "ghost" problem in chapter three. To refresh your memory, they received Christ and decided to sleep in separate bedrooms, turning completely to lives of celibacy until they could get married. We baptized them in bathtubs and rejoiced with them as we watched their lives transform before our eyes. The young man proposed within a month, and I was asked to officiate the wedding.

At first I was excited! We had seen God do such a work in this couple's relationship and individual lives. On the surface, it looked like a fairy-tale testimony. Nevertheless, a Word of Knowledge shook things up about two months later.

The Holy Spirit revealed something to me that only Jesus could know: these two shouldn't get married. I felt that their relationship was utterly wrong, even though everything looked so right.

For some reason, the Lord didn't reveal every detail—perhaps because He wanted me to walk out the process in a healthy way. I approached the groom-to-be and said, "If I'm going to officiate your wedding, I need to have peace about something. Forgive me if I'm totally off on this, but I get the sense that you two shouldn't be getting married."

The man took a deep breath and nodded his head. "Well, actually," he began, "I know we told you guys that I'm divorced, but I'm technically still married to my wife right now. We've been estranged for two years, and now we're just waiting for the paperwork to go through. What should I do?"

"Well," I answered, "You should call off the wedding and go patch things up with your wife."

"I haven't been on speaking terms with my wife in two years! How am I supposed to do that?"

I thought for a moment and replied, "Let's just ask the Lord to make it easy." Then we prayed together.

The next day, the bride-to-be got upset and stormed out of the house, saying she was leaving for good. There was step one. My wife, Robin, spent some time with her to walk her through the sudden chaos.

God likes to bring order out of chaos, though. Two days later, the man's actual wife called him—without knowing what was going on—and said, "I think we should patch things up."

Within a week, she had moved back in with him, and their marriage was restored. I was invited to come meet her for the first time, and that night she received salvation and was baptized in her bathtub! Then I prayed for both the husband and the wife to be filled with the Holy Spirit, and they received! Within another month, they renewed their vows and restarted their lives together, raising their two sons as a family.

At first glance, someone in the world might say that the Word of Knowledge I received was destructive—separating a lovely relationship between two Christians. But God is more powerful than that. God loves to find the darkest death and breathe resurrection life into it! In this case, the Word of Knowledge provided a turning point that set in motion a course of events that brought God far more glory than any of us could have imagined.

The Word of Knowledge is a powerful tool in ministry. Whether you're pastoring people, counseling them, or teaching them, the Word of Knowledge can accelerate the work of God and accomplish things that would otherwise be impossible. Every person in ministry should eagerly desire this gift.

Summary Questions

1. Why is it so important to wait to receive God's heart before acting on a Word of Knowledge?

_____

_____

2. List some reasons why the Word of Knowledge is such a necessary spiritual gift in the Church.

_____

_____

3. What ministry or ministries are you currently involved in? How could a Word of Knowledge be of help in that specific area?

_____

_____

4. Can you think of a ministry that would not benefit from someone receiving a Word of Knowledge? Why did you answer the way you did?

_____

_____

Endnote

1. This concept is mentioned in an audio teaching by John and Paula Sandford about "Small Groups" in *The Relationship Series*, which is available through Elijah House Ministries at www.ElijahHouse.org.

Chapter 8

pitfalls to avoid ↗

The enemy loves to attack those of us who have spiritual gifts because we are the most detrimental to his plans. Due to this, every spiritual gift has its potential pitfalls.

Before I start getting specific, I want to underscore the root of all the pitfalls, which is pride. If we do not deal with the self-life by crucifying ourselves with Christ, then we cannot receive the resurrection life of His Holy Spirit. (See Galatians 2:20 and Romans 6:5-10.) Receiving the power of the Holy Spirit without new life from the Holy Spirit tends to feed our egos rather than revealing Christ.

That's why the disciples struggled so much in Luke 9 with carrying the authority they were given. Until Jesus died, their sin couldn't die; and until God poured out His Holy Spirit, they were not able to receive His baptism. Instead, they continued to live out of their self-lives—arguing over who is the greatest, desiring to force people to accept them, and believing that they were the only ones who should be in ministry. (See Luke 9:6, 46, 49, and 54.)

Even Spirit-filled Christians struggle with pride. The Co-rinthian church was noted for the fact that they did not lack in any spiritual gift. (See 1 Corinthians 1:7.) However, only a couple of chapters later, Paul pointed out that they were still carnal because their pride was getting the best of them (in the form of envy, strife, and divisions). (See 1 Corinthians 3:3.)

We should not think that we are any more immune to pride than the Corinthians. Where spiritual gifts are pres-ent, the enemy plants magnetic landmines that have an un-shakable attraction to pride. Those of us who do not live in unity with Christ in His death and resurrection fall victim to the attack.

I recognize that there is a danger in exposing specific pitfalls. That danger is that some readers may focus on the pitfall rather than the root issue of pride. If you're wearing an iron suit in a magnetic minefield, it won't do you any good to pull ticking mines off yourself and try to throw them away. Nor will it do any good to try avoiding them. Take off the iron suit!

On the other hand, by admitting a struggle with one of the pitfalls, our pride gets exposed and can be dealt with more effectively. It's like when you go through a metal detector at an airport. You might think you put every bit of metal on the conveyor belt, but you may have forgotten about your watch. Consider the pitfalls I share to be "pride detectors." If you see yourself slipping up in an area, the solution is not to focus on that area itself. The solution is to deal with your pride by returning to the cross and putting it there with Christ.

Pitfalls to Avoid

With that in mind, let's take a look at what I will call the first common pitfall for those who practice the Word of Knowledge.

Acting Like You Know Everything

As soon as I started practicing the Word of Knowledge, people started looking at me differently. One friend of mine said he didn't want to hang out with me anymore because he was afraid that God would tell me all his secrets and he would be too embarrassed. I've heard other Christians talk about someone with this gift as though he or she were some sort of guru who "sees all and knows all."

If we have pride, it's very easy to start playing along with the assumptions of others. It's not hard to walk with a different posture, offer mystical glances, and speak vaguely to imply that you know more than you really do. All this brings plenty of glory to us, but little glory to Jesus.

Another form of this pitfall is finding out information from someone and responding as though it's not news to you—like God had revealed it to you already. If something doesn't surprise you, that's one thing; but it is a lie to act like God revealed it to you when in reality you only had an ordinary human hunch.

If you're going to practice this gift with authority from God, then you need to remain submitted to Him. Constantly give Him the glory. Be real with people by explaining exactly how you know what you know—rather than letting

161

them think that you have some psychic power to expose all their secrets.

Cheapening the Gift with Vague Intuition

Related to the first pitfall, this happens when we have a natural human hunch about something based on knowledge gleaned naturally.

For instance, you notice the way a man and woman talk to each other, and you get the feeling that they might be in a relationship. What do you do with that information? If one of those people is your friend, you might ask, "Is something going on between you two?" That's normal. However, it would not be right to say, "I think the Holy Spirit was showing me that you have feelings for each other." This is a lie because you didn't get that thought from the Holy Spirit; you got it from observation.

When we pick things up with natural human intuition, it is not right to pretend that we heard from the Holy Spirit. For one thing, it would be a lie, and for another thing, it cheapens the gift. Human intuition is often wrong in whole or in part, so to attach the name of God to it will cause people to mistrust your so-called revelations. Before long, they won't put much weight in what you have to say because they have not seen consistent accuracy.

Again, the root is pride—wanting to be seen as being more gifted than we actually are. But the result is that we're seen as less gifted. Only attribute things to God when you are certain that they are from God. You may fool people, but you won't fool Him; and His opinion is the only one that matters.

Saying More Than You Actually Know

Sharing a Word of Knowledge is like balancing on a tight rope—we have to step only where there's rope and constantly check our balance. If God only reveals one thing, just share that one thing—adding extra thoughts only muddies the water. The further we stray from the actual word, the more we lose our balance. Deviate from the word completely, and you're sure to fall.

A Word of Knowledge is not a person's life story. It is just a word (or single message). We only know in part. (See 1 Corinthians 13:9.) Don't feel obligated to have a huge revelation in order to be effective. If God only gave you one little thought, then that's because He knows that one little thought is all that you need.

This is especially true when the Word of Knowledge is related to dreams, visions, and their interpretations. It's very easy to add details to images that weren't really there, and it's also easy to look for meanings in symbols that God wasn't actually revealing. We have to walk the balancing act that keeps us focused on the actual revelation of God and not slip into the pitfall of sharing extra ideas.

In my experience, many times the Holy Spirit will only share a tiny bit of revelation with me and wait to see what I do with it. My pride wants to share a sermon-length message, but He only showed me one little thought. If I add to it, the person might walk away a little bit blessed. But if I'm faithful and only share the little bit, the Spirit will often share more within a few moments. Often times God wants to see what we will do with a few things before He entrusts to us many things. (See Matthew 25:21.)

Welcoming a Spirit of Divination

In Acts 16:16-19, we read about a slave girl who had a demon that enabled her to foretell the future. The slave owners were marketing her ability and earning money from her fortune-telling. When she saw Paul, Silas, and the rest of their entourage, she received what might have looked to many like a Word of Knowledge. The slave girl followed them for days and kept shouting, "These men are servants of the Most High God, who are telling you the way to be saved."(See Acts 16:17.)

As always, the root was pride. It is actually possible that this girl started out earlier in life with a genuine, God-given gift. But driven by the need to perform, she started to listen to any spirit that would give her information.

When we start to get performance-oriented and feel compelled to always have a "word," we open ourselves up to evil spirits. It doesn't matter if you're trying to please men or please God with your performance—the result is the same.

There's no need to perform to please God. When He opened the heavens over Jesus and said, "This is my most loved Son in whom I am well pleased," it was before Jesus had started His ministry or even worked one miracle. God is not looking for performers; He is looking for sons.

Likewise, there's no need to please man because that is of no eternal value. Who are you trying to impress? Why do you feel that you need to impress? It's pride, plain and simple, and it opens the door to a spirit of divination.

Furthermore, if someone comes to you asking for a Word of Knowledge, don't give them one unless you already have it. What they're really asking for is a sign to help them dispel their unbelief, but that's not how Jesus works.

The Pharisees came and began to question Jesus. To test him, they asked him for a sign from heaven. He sighed deeply and said, "Why does this generation ask for a miraculous sign? I tell you the truth, no sign will be given to it." Then he left them, got back into the boat and crossed to the other side (Mark 8:11-13).

When we try to please people and perform, we look for any stray voice that will help us out. Pride opens the door to evil spirits.

Marketing the Gift

Another thing that can give access to a spirit of divination is marketing the gift as if it were something to be peddled.

Marketing isn't necessarily a bad thing for the church. It's OK to invite people to events and services. It's even OK to say that you're going to expect the Holy Spirit to show up in power. But it's not wise to say definitively that the Holy Spirit will do this or that unless He specifically tells you to say it.

Why? Performance orientation! Just because you have a tendency to exercise a certain spiritual gift doesn't mean it will happen at every single meeting. What happens when everybody shows up expecting a Word of Knowledge and you have nothing to offer from the Lord?

Spiritual gifts are designed to function within the context of community. People should come to church to encounter God—not to see a circus act. When a spiritual family of believers collectively relies on the Holy Spirit to move in and through them, anyone stepping into their midst is sure to encounter God. It's not because anyone is performing; rather, it is because Jesus Christ is free to receive glory through His Body. Marketing the church or the meeting is one thing; but marketing a particular gift takes the focus away from the person of Christ and focuses it on one little part of His Body.

What would you do if you had traveled several hours to see your favorite recording artist perform; but when the artist came out on stage, he hid behind a curtain and held his finger over the top? No singing, no music. Just a finger. Would you be happy? In the same way, you're not the attraction—you're just one little part of Jesus. People should be attracted to Christ in the Church, not to you. If you want people to see the fullness of Christ, then don't market your gift as though it is the be-all-end-all of Christian ministry.

When I do a meeting, I make it a point not to promise any particular gift. If people want to come hear me speak or lead worship, that's fine; but I don't promise them anything other than my presence. If I did, it would pressure me to perform and meet expectations, potentially opening me up to a spirit of error. On the other hand, if I haven't promised anything, then I'm not required to perform, and the Holy Spirit is free to use me in whatever way He sees fit—teaching, healing, prophecy, music, miracles, exhortation, or Word of Knowledge.

Focusing on the Response of People

It is very easy to slip into a mindset in which you feed on the reactions of others. All it takes is one string of compliments to make you look for a pat on the back the next time you use your gift.

This can trap you in two ways. The first way is, again, performance-orientation. You could start trying to perform—not to please people or God, but simply to please yourself and stroke your own ego, always looking for the next compliment. The second way this can trap you is with discouragement. When you have this mindset, all it takes is one meeting when no one sings your praises. Suddenly, you find yourself feeling like nothing worked—possibly even drifting into depression.

The enemy is subtle like that. It is easy to slip into such pitfalls. Nevertheless, if we keep our pride in check, then we have nothing available for the enemy to snare. It is not your responsibility to get compliments; it is your responsibility to be an ambassador of Christ. Focus on Christ and revealing Him.

Fear of Failure

On the other side of all this is the tendency to remain silent. It seems like the opposite of the other pitfalls because it involves being quiet rather than rambling or saying too much. Nevertheless, it is still rooted in pride because it typically stems from a fear of failure or a desire to protect one's reputation.

We don't want to look bad. We don't want to mess up. We don't want to look like some sort of lunatic. We may say we don't want to hurt God's reputation, but really we're just trying to preserve our own! God can stick up for Himself, so don't worry about defaming Him. The issue is you.

Don't be afraid of messing up. The same God who once transformed dirty water into the best wine is still capable of smoothing over our rough edges. The key is simply that we operate in humility and crucify all pride. If your heart is to bring glory to God, then He'll get glory. People tend to have a lot more patience with those who are genuinely humble, and God has promised to exalt the humble in due time. Keep your focus on Him, and step out in faith. If your heart is right, there's no such thing as failure. If your heart is full of pride, then even your success is a failure. God opposes the proud and gives grace to the humble. (See James 4:6.)

Sharing the Word but Missing the Heart

As mentioned in the previous chapter, having a Word of Knowledge is great, but we must also receive the heart in which God intends it to be conveyed. If all you have is information, then you don't really "know" in the biblical sense of the word. Demons can convey information without any trouble, but only God can convey heart.

If you receive a Word of Knowledge, don't act on it until you have clarity about how God wants you to act. Ask Him for His heart on the matter and wait until you can see the person and the situation through the lenses of His perspective. You'll know you've got it when you feel overwhelmed with love for the person. Never act on a Word of Knowledge without love.

First Corinthians 13 goes into great detail about the love of God and how it relates to spiritual gifts. You could have the most detailed Word of Knowledge that God has ever given, but if you don't have love, it means absolutely nothing.

Those who share spiritual gifts without the supernatural love of God backing them up are loose cannons. Rather than targeting the enemy, such a person also risks wounding other believers. Those who shoot guns know that you have to take your time and focus your breathing in order to make a good shot. People tease me when I shoot skeet because I often wait until the clay pigeon is almost too far away to hit before I pull the trigger. They tease me, but I often shoot more skeet than them! In the same way, when we restrain ourselves and choose not to speak or act until we can do so in love, we more often find the ability to have pinpoint accuracy.

Apathy

The final pitfall I want to discuss is apathy. Many ministers find themselves no longer caring like they used to. There are probably thousands of superficial reasons for it to set in, but again the root is pride.

Apathy sets in when we stop putting others ahead of ourselves. Oftentimes it comes with a mindset that says, "I deserve a break." As soon as you start thinking about what you deserve, pride has already set in.

Apathy can also come from a lack of satisfaction with ministry. Satisfaction will wane if you start to believe that your spiritual gift is about you and your ability. Likewise, if you believe your gift is about others and how they receive it, you will quickly find yourself discouraged. It's not about you, and it's not even about others. If you want your gift to be perpetually fueled with passion, you must see it as a matter of obedience to the God you love. It's all about Him and no one else.

The only way to steer clear of apathy is to keep your focus humbly on God. Cultivate your relationship with Him. Spend time with Him in prayer, meditation, worship, study, journaling, and reading the Word. Engage in meaningful fellowship with other believers so that you can encounter Christ through the lives of others. It's all about Him.

Dealing with Pride

If you noticed any of the above tendencies in your life, then you probably have a problem with pride. If you did not recognize a problem with any of them, then you still have a problem with pride! Since we remain human beings, pride must be continually brought into submission to Jesus Christ. It is a daily, moment-by-moment choice. As soon as we think we're done dealing with pride, pride has already crept back in.

It may seem strange to try ridding ourselves of something that comes so naturally. However, pride is not natural. When Adam and Eve sinned, pride became the default for the human race; but anything that was not created by God is not natural. Pride is a perversion of the truth and seeks to distance men and women from the God who loves them. It is a tool of the enemy to take our eyes off of Christ and place them on ourselves.

We all have a problem with pride. Some have dealt with it more than others, but we all have to purposefully keep our sinful natures on the cross with Christ. This may sound contradictory, but the way to do that is to rest in Him. We fight through rest. We have to purposefully trust that His grace is sufficient and that His sacrifice was complete. Theologians call that "faith."

As soon as we start striving in our own strength and relying on our own ability to stay free from sin, we have already arisen in pride. Only Christ can set you free, and only Christ can keep you free. All we need to do is to offer ourselves to

Him. Notice in the following passage that all the required actions are summed up by simply making choices:

> *In the same way, count yourselves dead to sin but alive to God in Christ Jesus. Therefore do not let sin reign in your mortal body so that you obey its evil desires. Do not offer the parts of your body to sin, as instruments of wickedness, but rather offer yourselves to God, as those who have been brought from death to life; and offer the parts of your body to him as instruments of righteousness. For sin shall not be your master, because you are not under law, but under grace* (Romans 6:11-14).

Outside of what Jesus Christ already did, there is no physical action that can set you free from sin. It all comes down to offering yourself to God and continuing to choose Him. Once you give Him your life, the Holy Spirit comes and enables you to have self-control.

How will you use that self-control? To whom will you offer yourself?

Trust in Jesus Christ and the work He did on the cross. It's not about your effort; it's all about His. This is the necessary mindset for the Christian life, and it is therefore the framework needed to carry the power of the Holy Spirit.

Everyone seems to want the anointing of God, but few seem to want the cross that comes with it. Put your old life to death with Christ and receive the new life that comes from His Holy Spirit. Then you will be ready to rightly exercise Words of Knowledge.

Summary Questions

1. Look through the sub-headings of this chapter and make a list of all the potential pitfalls. Have you ever struggled with any of them? Are you currently struggling with any of them?

_____

_____

2. What are some ways that people often grant access to a spirit of divination?

_____

_____

3. How would you define "Performance Orientation"?

_____

_____

4. What is the solution for dealing with pride?

_____

_____

Chapter 9

activating and cultivating
the word of knowledge ↗

This is what the Lord says, he who made the earth, the Lord who formed it and established it—the Lord is his name: 'Call to me and I will answer you and tell you great and unsearchable things you do not know' (Jeremiah 33:2-3).

Have you ever taken the time to really think about that Scripture? God made it clear to the prophet Jeremiah that He would reveal unknown mysteries in response to human requests. The principle still applies today. If you want to practice the spiritual gift of a Word of Knowledge, the first key is to simply ask God for it. Call to Him, and He will answer!

Check your motives, though. If you want the gift for the wrong reasons, it won't work out. Either you'll find yourself slipping into the pitfalls of the previous chapter (due to pride), or else God won't give you the gift in the first place.

...You do not have, because you do not ask God. When you ask, you do not receive, because you ask with wrong

motives, that you may spend what you get on your pleasures
(James 4:2b-3).

If your heart is to reveal God's love and glory, then He invites you to call to Him. In response, He will reveal things you couldn't possibly know any other way. God loves to give good gifts to His children, and the gift of a Word of Knowledge is no exception.[1]

Ask and it will be given to you; seek and you will find; knock and the door will be opened to you. For everyone who asks receives; he who seeks finds; and to him who knocks, the door will be opened.

Which of you, if his son asks for bread, will give him a stone? Or if he asks for a fish, will give him a snake? If you, then, though you are evil, know how to give good gifts to your children, how much more will your Father in heaven give good gifts to those who ask him! (Matthew 7:7-11)

Ask, Seek, and Knock

This issue of "ask, seek, and knock" is essential for receiving a Word of Knowledge. Christians quote this verse a lot of the time, but we often overlook its context.

The verse is found in the two gospels of Matthew and Luke. In Matthew, as we just read, part of the context is in regard to asking God for gifts. But if you read the verses around that passage, you will discover that the fuller context has to do with ministering to others.[2] In Luke, we find a similar setting that gives even clearer detail:

Then he said to them, "Suppose one of you has a friend, and he goes to him at midnight and says, 'Friend, lend me three loaves of bread, because a friend of mine on a journey has come to me, and I have nothing to set before him.'

"Then the one inside answers, 'Don't bother me. The door is already locked, and my children are with me in bed. I can't get up and give you anything.' I tell you, though he will not get up and give him the bread because he is his friend, yet because of the man's boldness [other versions say "persistence"] he will get up and give him as much as he needs.

"So I say to you: Ask and it will be given to you; seek and you will find; knock and the door will be opened to you. For everyone who asks receives; he who seeks finds; and to him who knocks, the door will be opened.

"Which of you fathers, if your son asks for a fish, will give him a snake instead? Or if he asks for an egg, will give him a scorpion? If you then, though you are evil, know how to give good gifts to your children, how much more will your Father in heaven give the Holy Spirit to those who ask him!" (Luke 11:5-13)

As you can see, the context of this passage has to do with asking for bread for someone else. By reading Matthew and Luke together, we discover that this "bread" has something to do with "good gifts" that are directly related to the Holy Spirit.

Throughout Scripture, "bread" has a very clear metaphorical meaning. First we see Exodus 12, in which the unleavened bread of the Passover meal reveals the Body of Christ, which would one day be broken for all mankind. Then, in Exodus 16, we learn about the bread from Heaven, which Jesus said in John 6 represented Himself. Then we have Exodus 25, in which God described to Moses the table of the Bread of the Presence, where the priests were to eat in the presence of God. In this case, eating the bread was a matter of intimacy with God, which we can only have because of Jesus. In all three cases, the bread represents Christ.

Therefore, to ask for bread for someone else is to ask for Jesus to be revealed to that person. And since this has to do with "good gifts" from the Holy Spirit, we can expect that God will use us by giving us exactly the spiritual gift we need to reveal Him. Remember what you learned in Chapter One: Spiritual gifts take place when the Holy Spirit takes some aspect of Christ and makes it known to us.

Ask God for bread. Ask Him to give you some aspect of Jesus to share with someone. It's not for you to hoard for yourself, and it's not for you to pretend to own. Let people know that it came from God. The bread isn't for you; it's for your friend.

If it were for your own benefit, then you would be asking with wrong motives. Gifts of the Spirit are not for our own benefit; rather, they are for the common good of the Church. (See 1 Corinthians 12:7.) Instead, let your reason for asking be about ministering to others. You can be sure that God is pleased to give His children bread when they need some to share with a friend.

Persistence Pays Off

The teaching about asking for bread also makes it very clear that persistence is a key component. Therefore, we should be encouraged to keep on asking, keep on seeking, and keep on knocking.

Many times, I will be ministering to someone and sense that a Word of Knowledge would be beneficial to help bring a breakthrough. So I ask God for a Word of Knowledge. Sometimes it comes right away, and sometimes I have to keep on asking. Often, God waits in order to help me establish that I really want the message.

After you have read all the previous chapters, this may come as a surprise to you, but I often don't want a Word of Knowledge. Why? Because then I have to do something with it! My flesh likes fitting in with the crowd even though my spirit longs to minister to others. It's an inner battle with which every Christian needs to wrestle—in fact, it's the battle with pride that I mentioned in the previous chapter. By making me keep asking, God enlarges my desire. I then find myself so relieved to finally receive the word that I no longer care what my flesh wants. God often requires our persistence in order to help us overcome our flesh.

Whether I ask once or ask ten times, the Scripture is proven true. If you need bread for a friend, ask and you will receive.

Sometimes, though, the message is veiled. Sometimes it comes in the form of a vision or riddle that needs to be understood or figured out.[3] Once you have asked and received, it's time to seek and find. Look into the revelation God gave you and find the meaning. Trust the Holy Spirit within you to bring full clarity to the message from God. The symbols will begin to make sense, and you will have a peace in your heart that it is truly the voice of God.

Now that you have received the message and found the meaning, there's still one more step. Just because you have the message and understand it doesn't mean you have the right heart to present it. Getting the right heart comes from time spent in intimacy with God. It comes from encountering His presence and having dialogue about His thoughts and desires. So after you ask and seek, knock and the door will be opened to you. It is interesting to note that the man in the house could not hand his friend bread without opening the door. You don't really have bread until you have met the Giver face to face.

Everyone who asks receives; but often what we receive is only the raw ingredients. Everyone who seeks finds; but often what we find is the recipe for mixing it all together and making sense of it. What we need is for the door to be opened—the door to the oven of God's fiery presence, which changes us more and more into the image of Christ. We get to go in with the dough. Only after we have allowed the consuming fire of God to refine us are we able to emerge with edible bread that can nourish our friend.

This exact process doesn't have to happen every single time we receive a Word of Knowledge or revelation.

Sometimes it all happens at once. Furthermore, it may look different every time. Asking, seeking, and knocking can all take place in a matter of seconds as we give God the opportunity to complete what He has started before taking action on it. Other times, I have seen the process take two or three days or more. If God is not in a hurry to reveal His heart, then you should not be in a hurry to reveal the Word of Knowledge. Have the patience to wait on Him, and you will find that your timing is perfect.

Getting Started

Perhaps you're thinking, "All this is great, Art, but I've never had a Word of Knowledge. I've asked for one, but I've never received one. How do I get started?" Here are some pointers to help get the ball rolling with this spiritual gift.

First, if possible, spend time with people who already practice this spiritual gift. This has both natural and spiritual implications. In a natural sense, you'll see firsthand how it works. You'll see how the person delivers the message and some of the different ways they receive it. In a spiritual sense, sometimes we find it easier to experience God's power in certain ways when we are around other individuals who have already experienced breakthrough in that area.[4]

If you don't know anyone who practices this gift, don't worry—that's why I have gone into so much detail in this book. Consider your time spent reading to help meet this need. Nevertheless, time spent with an already-gifted person can be beneficial.

Second, and more importantly, you must be an active listener. When digging through rubble, rescue workers listen for the slightest sound and act on it. They can't afford to convince themselves that what they heard was nothing. If you're waiting for the sky to rip open and a voice to thunder from Heaven, think again! The still, small voice of God can be easily missed if we're not looking for it. If you have even the slightest hunch about something, and there's no natural explanation for it, you might have received an early form of the gift. God often tests how we will respond to little revelations before He gives us bigger ones.

This leads to the third piece of advice: Give it your best shot!

...Since you are eager to have spiritual gifts, try to excel in gifts that build up the church (1 Corinthians 14:12b).

Notice the words "try to excel." The word "try" means to actively attempt something. In essence, it means to give it your best shot! The Word of Knowledge is one of those gifts that can enhance ministry within the church in so many ways, so let's accept the scriptural mandate and "try to excel" in it. This means that as you actively listen for the slightest inkling of a Word of Knowledge, take action on whatever you sense. Like rescue workers trudging through rubble, listen for the faintest voice and go for it!

If you're anything like I was in the early days of practicing this gift, you'll find that a lot of times what you sense is nothing. But don't be discouraged! Thomas Edison is credited for saying that he didn't fail 700 times as he was trying to make his light bulb; on the contrary, he succeeded in finding 700 ways that don't work! As you're developing your gift, expect to find ways that don't work, and pay attention to them. This will help you weed out stray thoughts later in ministry.

Finally, to reiterate the first half of this chapter, keep on asking. Let God build your desire and passion for this spiritual gift as you seek Him with persistent petitions. Keep on asking, keep on seeking, and keep on knocking. Eventually, the Holy Spirit may take something Jesus Christ knows and make it known to you. You will have bread for your friend. God loves to give good gifts to His children, and He wants to give you Words of Knowledge more than you even want to receive them.

Summary Questions

1. In the parable of the man asking for bread for his friend, who did the bread represent? How does this relate to spiritual gifts like the Word of Knowledge?

   _____

   _____

2. Describe the process of "ask, seek, and knock" in your own words.

   _____

   _____

3. Why is persistence such a vital component in activating and practicing this spiritual gift?

_____

_____

4. What practical steps are you going to take as you "eagerly desire" this spiritual gift?

_____

_____

Endnotes

1. The two Scriptures just shared (from Jeremiah and James) are not specifically about the Word of Knowledge in context. On the contrary, they have far deeper implications. Nevertheless, they apply to this topic in principle and remind us how our Father in Heaven loves to reveal His knowledge to those who ask Him for it.

2. Specifically, read Matthew 7:1-12.

3. Numbers 12:8 shows that God sometimes speaks to people in riddles. In other words, He says things in a way that we need to figure out the meaning. As Proverbs 25:2 says in the New Living Translation, *"It is God's privilege to conceal things and the king's privilege to discover them."* See also Psalm 78:2.

4.   In First Samuel 10:10, Saul (soon to be "King Saul") walked into the midst of a company of prophets. When he did this, the Spirit of God came upon him and he started prophesying also. Later, in First Samuel 19:18-24, we read a story of King Saul sending wave after wave of soldiers to capture David (who was hiding with the prophet Samuel). But every time the men got near Samuel, they started prophesying! Finally, Saul decided to take matters into his own hands by going himself, but he too began to prophesy. Sometimes physical proximity to a person with a gift can somehow bring us into a spiritual atmosphere in which we begin to practice that same gift.

conclusion ↗

Now that you have a better understanding of the Word of Knowledge and how it can be implemented in the Church, imagine what could happen if everyone else in the Body of Christ knew what you know. What would happen if Christians in every ministry started to eagerly desire the Word of Knowledge and to exercise it in proportion to their faith?[1]

Now, please allow me to contradict myself for a moment. One of my pet peeves is people who have a particular spiritual gift and then try to convince the Church that every Christian needs that gift. Spiritual gifts are given by the sovereign will of the Holy Spirit—not taught. (See 1 Corinthians 12:11.) All children from a traditional American background know that they can learn about a toy for months, but they don't have it until they open the present on Christmas morning. In the same way, spiritual gifts can be learned about for decades, but only the Holy Spirit can "open" them up—bringing the gifts to life in a believer.

When a certain gift is taught as though every Christian needs it, the natural result is discouragement. We've seen this happen especially with the gift of healing. Christians who don't see God regularly healing others through their prayers often feel inferior to those who do. If we're not careful, biblical teachers can become sources of discouragement as they try to convince people that they need a particular gift in order to be truly valuable to God. This is not my intent. A right perspective of spiritual gifts is one in which we are perfectly satisfied with the gift or gifts that God gives us, and yet we eagerly desire additional gifts with fervency.

Consider, for instance, the gift of prophecy. Paul said, *"Follow the way of love and eagerly desire spiritual gifts, especially the gift of prophecy."* (See 1 Corinthians 14:1.) The Greek term rendered "eagerly desire" literally means to crave or even lust after. It implies a feeling of desperation and yearning. Several verses later, Paul continued, saying, *"...you can all prophesy in turn so that everyone may be instructed and encouraged."* (See 1 Corinthians 14:31.) We see a similar mindset coming from Moses, who declared, *"I wish that all the Lord's people were prophets and that the Lord would put his Spirit on them!"* (See Numbers 11:29.)

Paul and Moses agreed—in an ideal world, every believer would prophesy. Nevertheless, Paul also made it clear that not everyone has every gift. (See 1 Corinthians 12:27-31.) Rather, we are all different parts of Christ's Body. So while it would be great to have everyone prophesy, and while everyone should eagerly desire to do so, the fact remains that not every Christian does.

Does this mean that those who prophesy are somehow better Christians than those who don't? Of course not. Paul made that clear also. (See 1 Corinthians 12:14-26.) All it means is that we should all desire every spiritual gift, but we shouldn't feel superior or inferior based on what gifts we do or do not have. Your value to God is not found in your spiritual gifts but rather in the simple fact that you are His. God is less interested in what part of Jesus is revealed through you and more interested in the fact that Jesus is in you at all.

So when it comes to the Word of Knowledge, you now find yourself at an interesting place. I hope by this point in the book you are eagerly desiring this particular spiritual gift. If you haven't already received it, then I'm sure you're asking God for it. And if you have received this gift, you might be wishing your friends could experience how easy it is to hear from God in this way.

Like Paul's perspective on the gift of prophecy, I would like to point out how effective the Church would become if every Christian practiced the Word of Knowledge. That doesn't mean anyone is less of a Christian for not receiving; it just means that it's a great gift to have and should therefore be eagerly desired. As you have learned, this gift is beneficial and complementary to prophecy, visions, dreams, healing, intercession, evangelism, and numerous other forms of Christian ministry. It can be a powerful tool!

So imagine what would happen if your entire church actively demonstrated the spiritual gift of Words of Knowledge. How would it change your congregation? How would it impact your community? How would it transform your relationships? Would the Gospel spread more effectively? Would sin be dealt with in more effective ways? Would prayer meetings become more passionate? Would counseling be more effective?

The answer to all these questions is a resounding "yes," so take what you now know to your friends and family. Share with them what is possible through the Holy Spirit. Inspire them to begin to eagerly desire the Word of Knowledge. My desire is to see fresh life breathed into the Church as we recover the full measure of this spiritual gift.

The Word of Knowledge doesn't need to be a mystery. The enemy would love to keep the church in the dark—relying only on partial definitions, rather than knowing the full truth. But God is ready to lavish His gifts on His children. Call to Him, and He will answer and show you great and unsearchable things you do not know.[2]

Endnotes

1. Romans 12:6-8 shows us that various spiritual gifts are to be exercised in proportion to our faith. So even though the Holy Spirit may give several people the same gift, it will likely have several different expressions and intensities based on how well they know the voice of the Lord.

2. Adapted from Jeremiah 33:3.

About Art Thomas

Art Thomas and his wife Robin teach, train, and equip the Body of Christ for supernatural ministry through personal experience, sound doctrine, and practical application. They are available to help facilitate training seminars for your church, revival meetings, Weekend Transformation Retreats, Spirit-filled outreaches, and evenings of worship and ministry to the Lord.

With over a decade of practical experience, Art is credentialed for ministry through the Michigan District of the Assemblies of God and is happy to minister in any denominational or non-denominational setting around the globe.

Art may be contacted via email at Art@Supernatural Truth.com.

For more information, please visit:

www.SupernaturalTruth.com